D1717975

Landscape Urbanism *A Manual for the Machinic Landscape*
Mohsen Mostafavi, Christopher Hight, Lawrence Barth, Iñaki Abalos & Juan Herreros
James Corner, Florian Beigel & Philip Christou, Michel Desvigne, Jesse Reiser & Nanako Umemoto
Michael Hensel, Alejandro Zaera-Polo, Detlef Mertins, Keller Easterling, Ciro Najle
Architectural Association

Edited by Mohsen Mostafavi and Ciro Najle

Landscape Urbanism *A Manual for the Machinic Landscape*

AA publications are initiated by the Chairman of the Architectural Association, Mohsen Mostafavi.

Designed and produced by the AA Print Studio.

Printed in Spain by SYL.ES

ISBN 1 902902 30 0

Credits
p. 4 © Philip Christou, Architecture Research Unit. p. 5 (top) © John Blythe, Architectural Association Photo Library. p. 6 © Paul Dawson, Architectural Association Photo Library. p. 7 (left) © Aerofilm; (right) © Gérard Dufresne. p. 8 (top) © Clara Kraft, Architectural Association Photo Library; (bottom) © Paul Dawson, Architectural Association Photo Library. p. 79 (right) © Öffentliche Kunstsammlung Basel, Kunstmuseum (photo Martin Bühler).

A catalogue of AA Publications is available from
36 Bedford Square, London WC1B 3ES
www.aaschool.ac.uk/publications

Landscape Urbanism *A Manual for the Machinic Landscape*

Mohsen Mostafavi

Landscapes of Urbanism

Time seems to pass. The world happens, unrolling into moments, and you stop to glance at a spider pressed to its web. There is a quickness of light and a sense of things outlined precisely and streaks of running lustre on the bay. You know more surely who you are on a strong bright day after a storm when the smallest falling leaf is stabbed with self-awareness. The wind makes a sound in the pines and the world comes into being, irreversibly, and the spider rides the wind-swayed web.
DON DELILLO, 'THE BODY ARTIST'

We seem to have a clearer conception of what urbanism was than of what it is or what it will become. Modernism was abundantly transparent in its division of the components that made up the new city: housing, work, leisure, etc. These elements were thought to be all that was needed, and the masterplan provided the vehicle for holding these functions together while nevertheless ensuring that they remained distinct and apart.

The centralized state seemed incapable of the vision required to structure a new urbanism that might approach anything as complex as the multilayered, multifunctional and in many respects conflicting organization of cities that had developed over many centuries.

In the new city, everything had to be ordered and precise in its relationship to other functions. This would allow the plan to be implemented in distinct phases over time. There was little room for the uncertainty of chance encounter, or the unpredictability of the unplanned. Planning became synonymous with certainty; freedom was what it curtailed. Citizens' actions were – and are – being played out within spatial frameworks that serve to reduce any diversity of events and to control (and thereby reform) behaviour.

Camino de Santiago, Pamplona, Spain

Parc des Buttes Chaumont, Paris, Alphand, Barillet-Deschamps & Davioud, 1860

Opposite: Mussel-growing fields, Brittany, France

Planning per se is not the sole instigator of this conception of urbanism. Rather, a particular mindset – one that seeks to avoid chaos and conflict at all costs – provides the morality of these transparent and hygienic urban landscapes. Modernism's prescriptions on urbanism were encapsulated in the dogma of the Athens Charter, which was itself partly based on the mechanization and rationalization of Abbé Laugier's treatises on Enlightenment urbanism. According to Manfredo Tafuri, Laugier's theories demonstrated a twofold inspiration: '... on the one hand, that of reducing the city itself to a natural phenomenon. On the other, that of going beyond any a priori idea of urban organization by applying to the city the formal dimensions of the aesthetic of the picturesque.'

By the middle of the eighteenth century Laugier had declared in his *Observations sur l'architecture*:

Whoever knows how to design a park well will have no difficulty in tracing the plan for the building of a city according to its given area and situation. There must be squares, crossroads and streets. There must be regularity and fantasy, relationships and oppositions, and casual, unexpected elements that vary the scene; great order in the details, confusion, uproar and tumult in the whole.

The modern city, however, emphasized regularity more than fantasy and imagination, and order rather than tumult. And perhaps this is because there was yet another aspect of the landscape tradition that had remained unexplored: its temporal characteristics. The temporality of landscapes renders them forever incomplete, and this incompletion can be seen as an antidote to the implicit finitude of zoning.

The rationality of urban naturalism, championed in particular by Le Corbusier, through his dream of high-rise buildings amidst an expanse of urban parks, has been replaced by the dissolution of the distinction between city and countryside. Today the ubiquitous sprawl of suburbia is a primary characteristic of metropolitan areas.

Many cities also find themselves accommodating large leftover spaces of abandoned industrial and residential buildings that produce new and unexpected urban landscapes in the heart of the city. The disused railway tracks and goods yards of London's King's Cross, for example, have been the subject of numerous unrealized projects over the years. In Detroit,

Yee Wo Street, Hong Kong

new agricultural sites and farmlands have appeared in the middle of the city, where an enormous number of houses were demolished. These potent and somewhat surreal landscapes await further transformation.

In many instances the current, temporary uses of such sites already contain clues to the potential diversity of future activities they might contain. Indeed the nuances of this relationship between permanent and temporary programmes are one of the key factors in maintaining the dynamism of a city.

Despite the fact that in many circumstances the planning of additional buildings may form a necessary ingredient to the programming of such sites, they require an approach altogether different to the simple remedies of infill projects. The pattern of equilibrium in these areas has given way to an imbalance, a new pattern in which the relationship between the density of built and unbuilt areas has to be rethought over time. Many Dutch landscape architects and urbanists, for example, have already utilized techniques such as the densification of new residential developments in order to provide landscapes that will compensate for the lack of alternative forms of public space. Modernist planning has been revived, albeit under a new guise.

As a framework for the imagination, landscape produces new insights in response to the contemporary urban situation. It allows one to describe that territory in terms of an equal, although artificial, dialogue between buildings and landscapes. Yet this dialogue is not limited by the traditional definition of the terms 'building' and 'landscape'; it allows for the simultaneous presence of the one within the other, buildings as landscapes, landscapes as buildings. And in this lies the potential to redefine the parameters of each discipline – architecture and landscape architecture – in relation to the other. By forcing us to rethink fundamental questions such as 'What is a building?' and 'What is a landscape?', these new hybrids add to the existing repertoire of material elements with which we construct future urbanisms.

But what is the relationship of urbanism to landscape in this context? On the one hand, one might see it as a literal transposition of the techniques and vocabulary of one to the other; and on the other, this relationship might operate on a metaphoric and metonymic register. The fact that urbanism relies as much on the construction of surfaces and voids as it does on the construction of buildings seems to make the literal use of landscape as a material device a

Northern Outfall sewage works, London

Urban development zone, Arcueil, France, Alexandre Chemetoff necessity. But at the same time, the fact that landscape architecture contains an explicit recognition of the changing nature of the land through time allows the possibility of a productive relationship on a metonymic register to an urbanism whose conception of time has generally become more implicit and linear.

The correlations between landscape and urbanism do not have to be limited to Tafuri's reading of Laugier, in which the city is 'reduced' to a natural phenomenon. For like cities, landscapes are cultural, social and political agents whose role is not exhausted by their formal and aesthetic performance. After all, even the picturesque tradition possessed social and cultural parameters to parallel its aesthetic concerns. In these terms it is the aspect of landscape that takes into account duration and time that reinforces our understanding of how the city lives, and the lives that are lived through it. According to Bergson, duration is a transition, '... a change, a becoming, but it is a becoming that endures, a change that is substance itself'. Duration is not 'merely lived experience; it is also experience enlarged or even gone beyond; it is already a condition of experience'.[1] Experience, however, involves a combination of space and duration. In actuality, space is often an interruption, a form of discontinuity, to the continuous nature of duration in its pure form.

Landscape urbanism consists of both a longer and a shorter timescale than that of building construction. It is longer like a tree that grows old, and it is shorter in its heightening of the ephemeral and its speed of transformation. Its speculations on the spatialities of everyday experience prevent it from the all-too-common assignation of meaning to forms. Rather, this approach aims at a search for the hidden pockets of potential, for opportunites in places where previously there were thought to be none. Consequently the urban surface becomes a site of new and unexpected events. The methods of landscape urbanism are operative, they prioritize the way in which things work and the way in which they are used. And like a landscape architect, the landscape urbanist always begins with the given.

This shift, from an image-based planning process to an operative method, is akin to the shift from the theories of the picturesque to the productive operations of agricultural territory. Even though such a territory possesses a visual dimension, its visuality does not dominate its daily procedures; it enables them and is a reflection of them. The agricultural field is ploughed, prepared in anticipation of the crop that will (hopefully) appear at a later date. In this way the

Barcelona beachfront and promenade, Olga Tarrasó

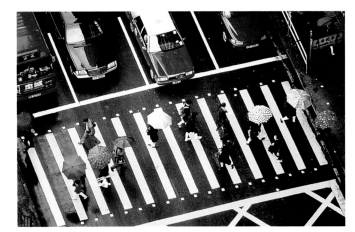

Causeway Bay, Hong Kong

1 Gilles Deleuze, *Bergsonism* (MIT Press: 1966), p.37.

appearance of the field is always both incomplete and complete, in as much as at each stage of its development it attains a certain degree of temporal finitude. The tension between the systemic nature of operative procedures and the contingent conditions of a site precludes contextualism as a localized form of operation. The rules of the operative system incorporate both material and immaterial logics, affected by the network of forces both near and far, both local and global.

In keeping with this, more recent ideas in urbanism rightly pay greater attention to the role of external forces in the shaping of our cities. These forces range from planning regulations to the opening and closing times of international financial markets, and they are physically transforming the contemporary city. An openness to these forces leads us towards a range of previously unforeseen programmes that, in turn, have an impact on the design of the urban fabric and can lead to a more intensive use of many urban districts.

But should urbanism be limited to a project that only responds to the given forces of a site (whether financial or regulative)? A consideration of urbanism in terms of the networks and infrastructure of a larger landscape should not only bring to bear the utilitarian aspect of these projects (railways, roads, pavements) but their reflexive and pleasurable responsibilities (scenery, driving, walking). Furthermore it suggests the need for the reconsideration of all the material elements (physical/conceptual, permanent/ephemeral) that together provide the infrastructure of the urban: highways, roads, rivers, bridges, embankments, paths, surfaces, lights, markings, signage. Given the disproportionate concern of contemporary urbanism with commerce and retail, these elements provide new opportunities for the redefinition of the public sphere. Instead of a nostalgic yearning for lost models of public space, monuments, piazzas, we should imagine, support and construct alternative models of urbanism that are open to, and encourage, participation by all citizens.

Landscape urbanism can be the catalyst for this transformation, since it addresses the larger urban territory that invariably combines both private and public ownership (rather than a series of isolated, privately owned setpieces, as is often the case with contemporary urban design). We cannot describe our societies as democratic without considering the spatial frameworks that enable democracy to act. Landscape urbanism will in future, with its temporal and political characteristics, set the scene (albeit momentary) for democracy in action.

FRAMEWORK ▸

The Architectural Association's graduate programme in Landscape Urbanism endeavours to incorporate the processes and techniques that have historically modulated the landscape into the domain of urbanism, empowering its ability to cope with the wide range of scales, the diversity of domains and the rapid changes at which it is currently being challenged to operate. Landscape urbanism develops methods for effectively synthesizing constraints from different disciplines and domains of production into an operative framework, absorbing knowledge that ranges from environmental engineering and landscape studies to urban strategy and the development industry. Yet it exceeds hybridization, as it simulates environmental, social and economic processes in abstract systems of relationships, attempting a shift from teleological programming to open diagramming, from techniques of imposition to techniques of interposition, from ideological positions to a fluent yet consistent browsing across contingency, and from the deliberate manipulation of typological configurations and regulatory conventions to the systematic management of virtually open relational assemblages. The understanding of landscape is central to this project, as it allows the integration of natural processes and urban development into the unfolding of an artificial ecology.–Ciro Najle

Fluctuant Compensations

The mix of local circulation and through-traffic is integrated into a spine of development. Its hourly fluctuations activate a differential use of the parking surface. The changing pollution levels this introduces are locally counterbalanced by a strategy of plantation of fluctuating density.

Frven Lim
Loop/Pool

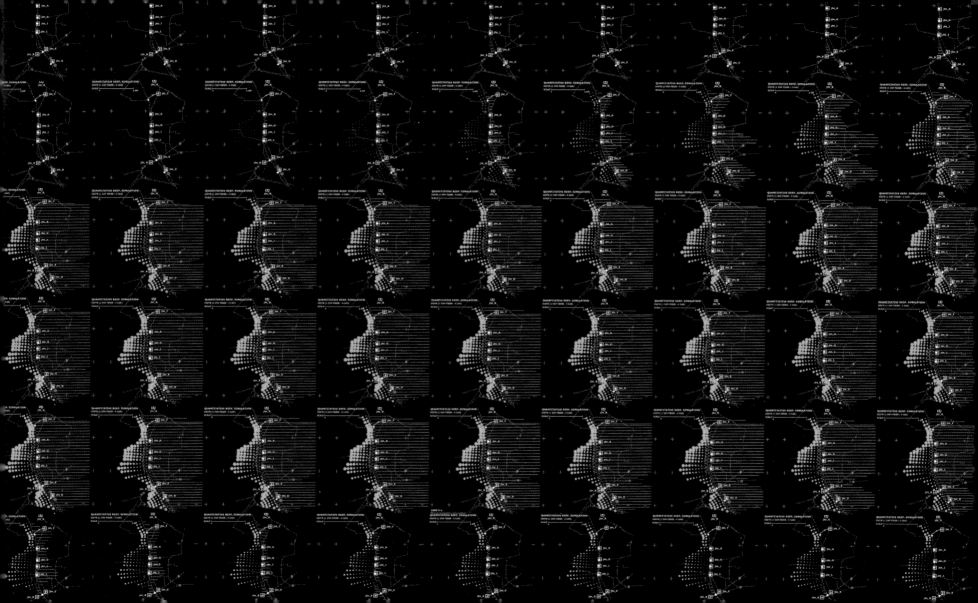

Combing Trajectories

A set of parallel pedestrian trajectories connects a spine with its immediate context at regular intervals. Traced across a field of infrastructural corridors, the trajectories are loaded with responsive mechanisms to moderate their impact.

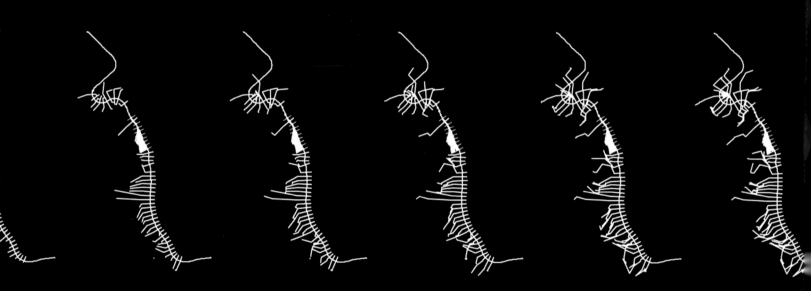

Julian Varas
Inhabiting the Artificial Ground

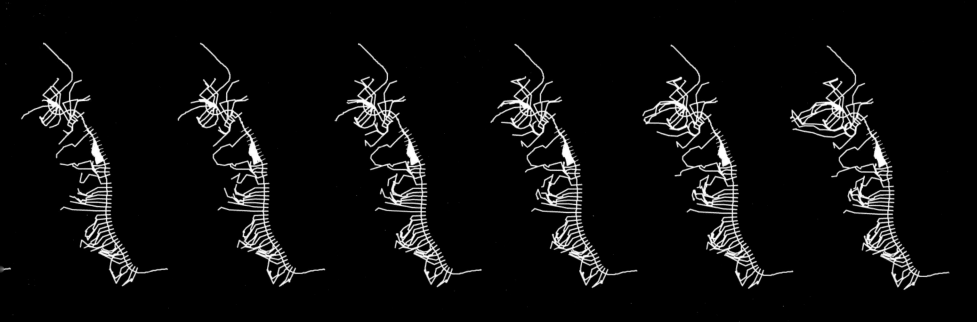

Catchment Network

The logistics of distribution of a chain of supermarkets regulates a network of catchment areas that reconfigure the relationship between infrastructure and derelict land.

Rosalea Monacella
Coexistive Territories

Lea Valley

Network

Filter derelict sites

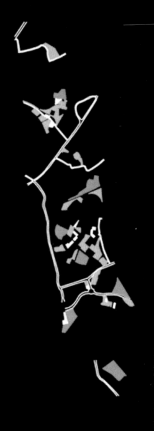

Derelict site potential

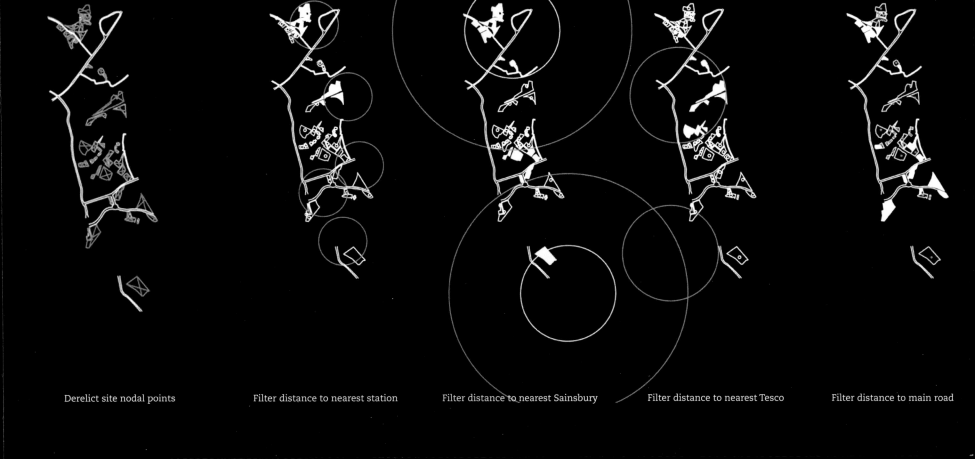

Derelict site nodal points   Filter distance to nearest station   Filter distance to nearest Sainsbury   Filter distance to nearest Tesco   Filter distance to main road

Bundled Network

Programmatic components are created as generic segments with extruded typical sections. They are arranged in parallel sets, flattened and accumulated around the nodes of an operational network. The accumulation progressively takes over available plots and links to the surroundings. The resultant network saturates the capacity of the site, forcing restrictions to operate as creative removing tools.

Rosalea Monacella
Coexistive Territories

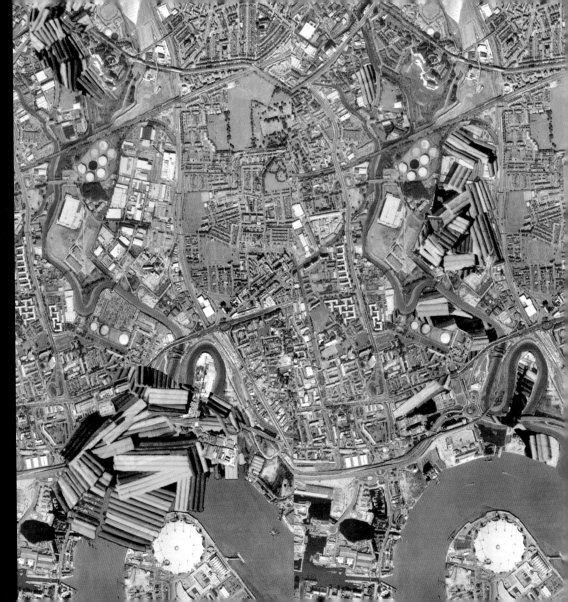

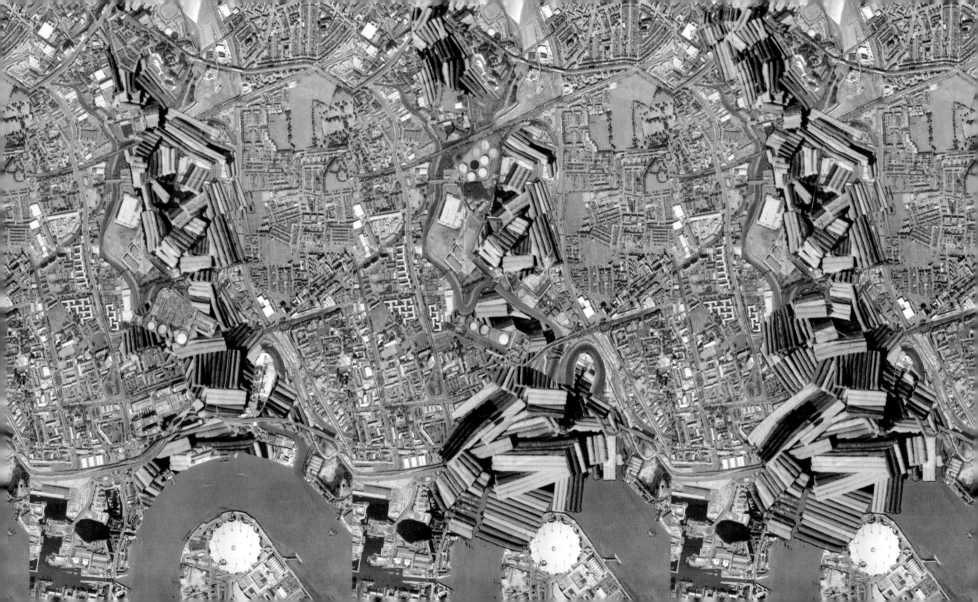

Blurred Network

The dichotomy between nodes and links disappears in a field that manages centralities by treating them as tendencies. A network spreads laterally and blurs in its immediate surroundings. The organization switches from a modality of nodal connectivity into a modality of distribution of transitions.

Intensive Shredding

A circulatory network transverses a shredded ground, activating it locally and introducing services, patios and vertical connections. The fabric switches from a modality of regular subdivision by modular repetition into a modality of differential terracing.

David Mah
Surface Matters

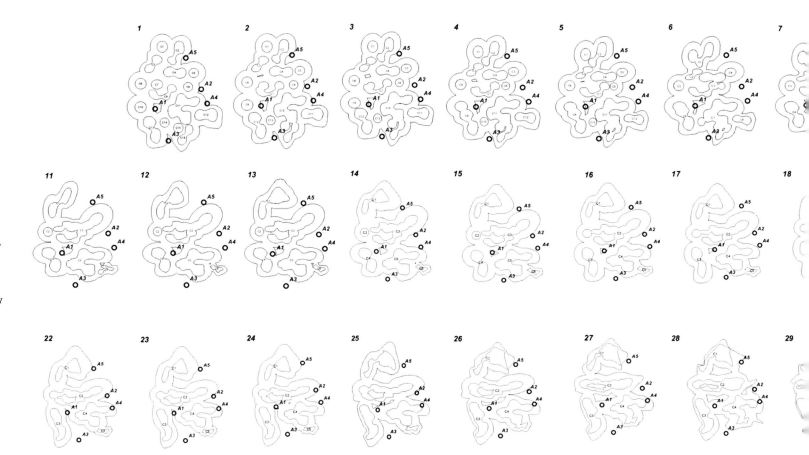

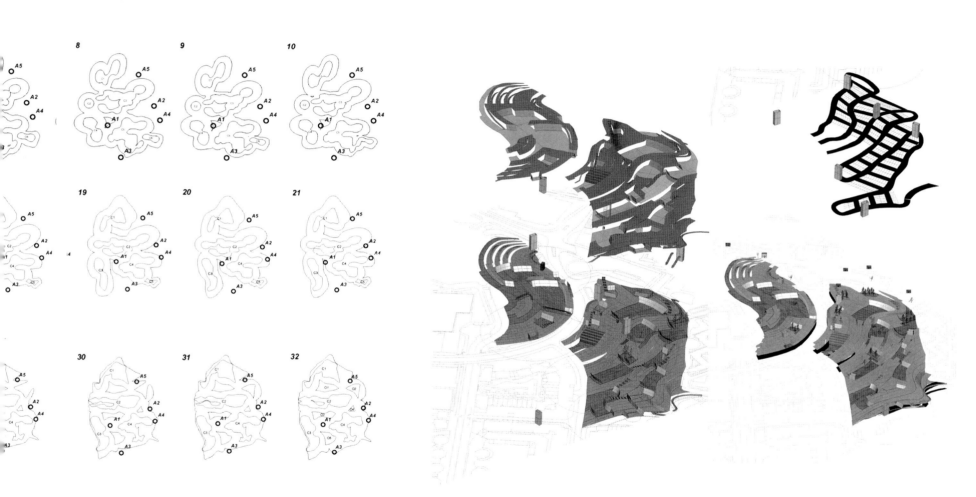

Fuzzy Network

Through the disruption of its straight-linearity, the widening of its section and the diversification of its material characteristics, a circulatory network constructed upon right-of-way segments traverses the postindustrial fabric and settles as a parallel leisure system.

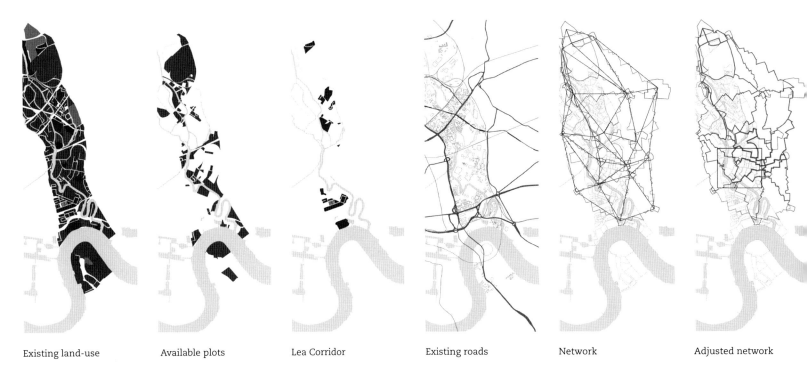

Existing land-use   Available plots   Lea Corridor   Existing roads   Network   Adjusted network

Fabian Hecker
Emerging Public Spaces

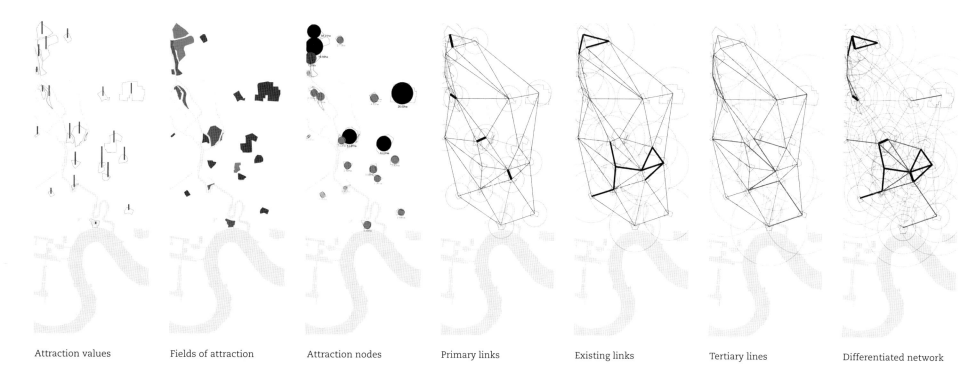

Attraction values   Fields of attraction   Attraction nodes   Primary links   Existing links   Tertiary lines   Differentiated network

Christopher Hight

Portraying the Urban Landscape: Landscape in Architectural Criticism and Theory, 1960 – Present

Miss X claims that she no longer has a brain or nerves or chest or stomach or guts. All she has left is the skin and bones of a disorganized body. These are her words.

JULES COTARD, 1891[1]

The Ethos of Landscape

Landscape urbanism ultimately suggests neither a new formalism nor a renewed emphasis on landscape in the city. It is not a theory of design, but promises to innovate at the level of *design practice*. It has emerged from a perceived crisis in which the traditional disciplines of architecture and urbanism are thought to be incapable of engaging the contemporary built environment. The urban milieu has altered so drastically in the past 50 years that the objects of architectural and urban knowledge – such as the 'city' – no longer exist as objects accessible to those fields. This is reflected in our terminology: we have moved from the city and suburb to what Paul Virilio calls the 'exo-city', something defined largely by what it is not, an exterior rather than a stable referent defined by a given body of knowledge. Like the shift from natural history to biological science in the nineteenth century, engaging with the recently emerged questions and problems requires a new organization of practice and knowledge. Only by producing new fields, methods and objects might we be able to understand the contemporary postmetropolis as a coherent entity. Thus, beneath the renewed interest in landscape lies an implicit assertion that bringing the design practices of urbanism and architecture into contact with that of landscape will rejuvenate all three. Previous professional identities and closed fields of knowledge are to be reformulated as a continuous landscape of transdisciplinary encounters, which in turn opens up new terrains of knowledge and possibilities for action.

1 Translated by Brian Massumi.

In this way, landscape urbanism offers, to use an unfashionable and misunderstood term, a design ethic. By this I do not mean a moral code, a legal standard or a 'green' mantra. Instead, I refer to ethos: a way of doing and a mentality which privileges certain values, norms, assumptions and methods, and which treats particular problems in particular ways. Most importantly, the ethos determines the way in which questions are asked. An ethos is not a definition or identity but a consistency in the manner of being, a mode of operation.

Moreover, landscape urbanism seems to require a certain type of ethos. Through his studies in the history of sexuality, Michel Foucault argued for the 'disassembly of the self' (*se déprendre de soi-même*), a position reiterated by Deleuze and Guattari in *A Thousand Plateaus*. In spite of its formalist reception in architecture, this text is mostly an instruction manual on how to 'make yourself a "body without organs"'. Making oneself a body without organs is similar to Foucault's *déprendre*: a freeing, distancing or, more precisely, disassembling of the essential humanist subject.[2] Both require turning from a molar (essentializing, unified) humanist identity to molecular (differential, multiple) assemblages. Such disassembly occurs not by critique or deconstruction but by becoming other (an example Deleuze and Guattari provide is the 'becoming animal'). All these becomings and bodies without organs, Deleuze and Guattari argue, prompt a shift from an ethics based on a 'logic of the same', projecting a normative model of identity, to an ethics of difference and assemblage. To return to a Foucauldian formulation, such 'becoming' enfolds the interior of thought with the previously unknowable virtualities lurking on its exterior. They see the 'logic of the same' as a Platonic mode of thought that projects a normative but ideal model as the real, against which all things are judged as good resemblances (copies) or bad simulations (simulacra). Simulations are not bad copies, but those things which cannot be recuperated into a mimetic economy of the 'same' as model-copy. The 'body without organs', the 'becoming animal', the *se déprendre de soi-même*, are such simulacra. They undermine the power of the 'logic of same' to fashion subjects as resemblances of an ideal normative model. The point is not to shift from one identity or resemblance to another but to employ simulacra to undermine the entire model-copy economy of resemblance.

Whatever difficulties there may be with such a formulation, and even though Foucault and Deleuze and Guattari were speaking of the identity of the self in society, this ethos can be

2 This is why Foucault called Deleuze's work a guide to nonfascist living.

applied equally to the transdisciplinary project of landscape urbanism and the identity of disciplines. Architecture traditionally operates through an ethics of stasis, truth, wholeness and timelessness; urban planning operates via control, determinism and hierarchy. In contrast, landscape design appears to offer an ethics of the temporal, complexity and soft-control with a commensurable spatial and organizational repertoire. It supposedly disassembles the identity of the architect and the urbanist and opens their fields of knowledge to 'other' potentials. Landscape urbanism, if it is to be anything, must be understood as an attempt 'to constitute a kind of ethics [as] an aesthetics of existence'.[3]

To assess what is at stake in such an endeavour, I want to highlight the complex relationship architecture and urbanism have enjoyed with the idea of landscape, as well as the irreducibly complex conditions of landscape as a mode of operation. Landscape design cannot simply become a new model. Firstly, it shares a problematic genealogy with painting, over-determined by the picturesque and the pictorial. As a result, landscape has operated as a dangerous simulacrum opposed to the model of architecture. The simple inversion of this relationship leaves the polarization intact. In tacit recognition of this problem, the conversion of landscape design into a model for urban design is often accompanied by a shift in the idea of landscape from the picturesque to the operative. However, the attempt to remove the pictorial sensibility of landscape conserves the ethos of architecture, one which is highly suspicious of representation while at the same time wilfully oblivious to its function as its own model. Instead of rejecting, or rather repressing, the pictorial aspects of landscape and its debt to painting, I will offer a different genealogical reading that embraces this past as a means to dissemble the identity of architecture as model. In short, I would argue that a coherent discourse on landscape urbanism cannot be sustained simply by elevating landscape as a new model, for it is the ethos of the model and copy itself that must be problematized.

Landscape as Simulation: The Colonial Gaze of Architecture

The encounter between architecture and landscape design is not new. Marc-Antoine Laugier suggested that designing a park was fair preparation for city planning. Here, landscape design served as a training simulation for urban design practices.

However, during the twentieth century, the two fields were related through an odd

3 Michel Foucault, 'On the Genealogy of Ethics', in *Ethics: Subjectivity and Truth, 1954–84* (New Press: 1997), p. 254.

epistemological 'orientalism' whereby landscape design functioned as architecture's adjacent other.[4] Landscape was something to tart up a plan: provide relief from urban congestion (Central Park); 'humanize' its rationalism (Ville Radieuse); or otherwise soften the cold, hard logic of the architect or planner. However, while landscape was the object of the architect's discursive wanderlust, to his 'colonial' eye it appeared rather uncultured, indeed wild. If a discipline requires rules, logic and method, landscape design did not qualify.

Reyner Banham, for example, argued that while English landscape painting was a singular contribution to art, no such claim could be made for English landscape architecture.[5] Banham even avoids the term 'landscape architecture', referring only to the 'landscape movement' or 'scene', as if it were a hip counterculture. Lest we mistake this as tacitly endorsing landscape as radical politics, it is clear that for him not only is landscape design not art, neither is it a discipline or even a profession. Instead, landscape design is merely the constructed resemblance of landscape painting, not an autonomous practice.

In one sense perhaps Banham was correct. The concept of landscape as such was formulated in painting, and only later deployed in actual parks, nature and cities. If architecture refers to an origin in the body or primitive shelter – in other words, to a natural order – landscape finds a less authoritative origin myth in painting. Landscape design was a copy of painting, which was itself a copy. All landscapes, it might be argued, are profoundly picturesque.[6]

The ethos at work in Banham's negative inferences and his focus on landscape's origins in painting are telling. There is an implicit analogy between the inferiority of the landscape architect to the landscape painter and Banham's later distinction between the designer of good buildings and the architect proper (Banham's iconoclastic example is Hawksmoor-the-architect versus Wren-the-nonarchitect).[7] A designer depicts architectural order but does not operate as an architect at the level of order. It is the mode of operation that defines a discipline, he argues, rather than any quality of beauty, function or other such criteria.[8] The difference is that the designer merely attempts to represent the appearance of order, the truth function, the logic, that is actually installed by real architecture or in painting. His distinction is therefore primarily ethical rather than epistemological or aesthetic. The ethos of the designer makes reproductions, shadows, rather than models of order.

4 I use the term 'orientalism' in the manner of Edward Said, as the 'other' which plays a constituent part in constructing the identity of the imperial power. Obviously, however, I am taking a liberty in giving this an epistemological and disciplinary function.
5 Reyner Banham, 'Kent and Capability', in *A Critic Writes* (University of California Press: 1996); originally published in *New Statesman* 64 (7 December 1962), pp. 842–3.
6 Of course, architecture is an image of architecture before it is anything else.
7 Banham, 'A Black Box: The Secret Profession of Architecture', in *A Critic Writes* (1996); originally published in *New Statesman and Society* (12 October 1990), pp. 22–5.
8 For Banham, the interior of architecture is an obscure 'black box' or 'inner sanctum'; it is harder to say what it is than to recognize objects and practitioners who are not 'it'. For him, it is even possible to be a singular genius or masterbuilder and yet not participate in architecture as a discipline (think of Gaudí or, apparently, Wren). In this regard, Banham allows a few isolated examples of landscape design to be designated as 'art'.

This analogy becomes more evident in Banham's description of Wren's St Paul's as 'the finest piece of urban scenography ... but please don't call it architecture'.[9] For Banham, St Paul's serves as a picture of urbanism but does not operate urbanistically or architecturally. Wren is contrasted not only to Hawksmoor but also to the strictly architectural Mies, who operates at the level of organization and 'rational explanation'.

English landscape architecture is, to his eye, similarly scenographic, like a portrait of a landscape but almost without exception a purely retinal resemblance rather than an original artwork in its own right. Just as a designer copies architectural order by making a picture of that order rather than operating within it, a landscape designer attempts to depict a landscape painting. It is for this reason that Banham cannot accord landscape design the status of artistic discipline. And it is even more problematic than architectural design, since that which Wren copied was architecture as model of natural order, while that which landscape design attempts to imitate is itself a resemblance, a painting. As a second-generation copy, landscape design appears as a simulacrum of a discipline. Though he does not put it in such terms, for Banham such simulacral practice can only be a false ethics.

The Operative Landscape

Banham's portrayal of landscape articulated a general intuition in architectural discourse. Reacting to the suspicion of its relationship with painting, landscape design has attempted to purge its pastoral and pictorial referents. In a recent article, Alex Wall argued that 'the term landscape no longer refers to prospects of pastoral innocence but rather invokes the functioning matrix of connective tissues that organized not only objects and spaces but also the dynamic processes and events that move through them'.[10] He further argues the need for this shift because the 'nature of the city' itself has become unprecedentedly formless, dynamic and complex. The objects of traditional architectural knowledge, he suggests, have been supplanted by undifferentiated expanses of surface organization. Wall concludes that one reason landscape is especially useful is its emphasis on the plan and the horizontal as an ordering surface: 'all things come together on the ground'.[11]

Yet how different is this from Le Corbusier's plan as generator of order? We should recall architecture's vast self-appointment as model for rational thought or natural order. A central

9 Banham (1996), p. 299.
10 Alex Wall, 'Programming the Urban Surface', in *Recovering Landscape*, James Corner, ed. (Princeton Architectural Press: 1999), p. 223.
11 Wall (1999), p. 247.

part of its status as model, as Banham's case reveals, is that architecture does not simply represent things but operates at the level of organization itself. That is to say, architecture is thought not to represent or be a picture of order but to serve as a model for order. If the nature of the city has changed, landscape is now being offered as a replacement model of order. To posit a shift to landscape design on the grounds that it allows access to the reality or new nature or essence of the city replays what has always been claimed as the task of architecture. The supposed shift to the operational attempts to recover landscape from its pictorial and innocent pastoralism, while leaving architecture and planning's underlying assumptions – namely, a deep suspicion of pictorial representation as simulacrum – intact. Thus, elevating landscape design to the status of model by stripping it of its problematic past merely conserves the ethics of an architecture based on the model-copy, in which it is urban design's task to copy the natural order of the city.

Landscape as General Theory

In any case, we can see how the recent reclaiming of landscape design from simulacrum to model is poised around two seemingly incompatible understandings. The first treats landscape as representation, depiction, mimesis and resemblance; the other concerns territory, encoding, transformations and dynamics. One is landscape as painted, the other landscape as occupied by forces and gang warfare. However, this division of landscape is inherently unstable. James Corner has argued that landscape inevitably entails both aspects as an eidetic projection of possibility.[12] But is it a visual (or other sensory) image of landscape that is being projected or something else that allows our recovery of landscape as an image of design practice?

Take, for example, Sanford Kwinter's seminal 1992 article 'Landscapes of Change'.[13] This text situates Umberto Boccioni's triptych *Stati d'animo* (1911) within the more recent epistemology of catastrophe theory and embryology. By reintroducing architecture to morphogenesis and nonlinear science, this article was central to the emergence of landscape design as a new mode for architectural practice. Kwinter described Boccioni's paintings as 'modal' landscapes of 'spatiotemporal' loci, intensities and forces, and in his conclusion argues for a renewed 'modal' approach to design. This modal design implicitly offers different

12 James Corner, 'Eidetic Operations and New Landscape', in *Recovering Landscape*, Corner, ed. (1999).
13 Sanford Kwinter, 'Landscapes of Change: Boccioni's Stati Re-producing Landscape d'animo as a General Theory of Models', in *Assemblage* 19 (1992), pp. 52–65.

ways of approaching reality and representation alike (opposed to the 'hylemorphic' and Platonic sensibilities of classical, and much of modernist, aesthetics). Part of this modal design is what Greg Lynn would later call an 'ethics of the animate', which takes the dynamic and the multiple rather than the static and the whole as premises of order.

Throughout the article this mode is defined through landscape, which operates as both an explicit trope and an operative strategy. It functions discursively as an analogy to topology, both surface organizations rife with heterogeneous transformations and multiplicity. Ontologically, two specific scientific models are analysed as event landscapes: Conrad Waddington's 'epigenetic landscape' and René Thom's 'catastrophe surface of capture'. Both of these subsequently became leitmotivs of architectural discourse. Epistemologically, it is as an analogous landscape of change, or more specifically Lucretian morphogenesis, that Kwinter diagrams Boccioni's painting. At the discursive level, therefore, landscape operates as a diagrammatic machine by which diverse fields of knowledge may be diagrammed upon a single surface. It was this 'general theory of models' as morphogenetic landscape that architecture attempted to emulate for the next ten years.

Yet while Kwinter employed landscape as operational mode, he also employed another sensibility of landscape, the representational and pastoral one. The argument, especially in its use of landscapelike images, is presented largely by asserting the resemblance of the painting to natural and scientific formations; processes of formation are dealt with extensively, but no link is made to Boccioni's process of painting. *Stati d'animo* is at once produced by a landscape modality and depicts such a landscape of 'transformational events'. The conclusion states that 'what we find depicted are three eventual complexes, or *three morphogenetic fields*', but also that 'each is *triggered* by a different singularity … incarnating the multiple conflictual play of forces' [my emphasis].[14] Which is it? Painting produced by the triggering of events or painting depicting events that occurred elsewhere? A picture of a modality or a modality that produces new pictorial sensibilities? Indeed, for architecture the presentation of a painting as a general model might itself be seen as conflicting with the intended shift to modal rather than representational design practices.[15]

Such instabilities emerge from the inherent complexity built into landscape as a mode of design. This is as integral to the idea of *Stati d'animo* as a morphogenetic landscape as it is to

14 Kwinter (1992), p. 63.

15 It should be noted that the article was originally intended for and published within the institutions of the visual arts and only afterwards republished in *Assemblage* as 'important for the journal's emerging programme' (Editor's note, p. 52). In that regard, the difficulty I am pointing out emerges in the article's appropriation.

Waddington's picturing of morphogenesis as a landscape. In fact, contemporary scientific discourse is populated with a litany of such tropes: Waddington's 'epigenetic landscapes', Kaufman's 'fitness landscapes', Thom's 'catastrophe landscapes', Uexhil's 'environmental capture'. In these sciences, an ethos of landscape offers an aesthetic schema for a different ontology in which it becomes possible to formalize different types of existence, different sorts of objects and new relationships between them. It is not simply that the material nature of cities has changed; these changes are perceptible and conceptualized as such only because of a reconfiguration in our formal schema of existence. Likewise, it is not simply that the objects of architectural knowledge have become dynamic surfaces of multiplicity, but that the aesthetic of the surface has become an epistemological site for reconfiguring architectural ethics. Landscape becomes possible as a mode of urban design only within this specific configuration of concepts, conditions and cross-disciplinary practices.

To understand this complexity in the image of landscape and to avoid reducing it either to a natural phenomenon or a sensorial representation, we might refer to its genealogy within modern aesthetic theory. In one of his early works, Walter Benjamin formalized their relationship: 'We should speak of two cuts through the world's substance, the longitudinal cut of painting, and the transversal cut of certain graphic productions. The longitudinal cut seems to be that of representations, of a certain way it encloses things. The transversal cut is symbolic, it encloses signs.'[16]

As Rosalind Krauss has noted, this formulation has pervaded the discourse of modern art and visual theory, traceable from Benjamin through Clement Greenberg and Leo Steinberg.[17] In art theory, the longitudinal cut is treated as the vertical, and the transversal as the horizontal. We can see that, under such a formulation, landscape painting offers a vertical representation of that which is organized along the transversal plan of signs.

Such a distinction is a convention of architectural drawing: the vertical facade and the transversal plan. However, here it is not a matter of simply contrasting horizontality with verticality; these cuts do not determine what can occur upon them in an essentialist manner. Instead, they mark two different modalities. Steinberg, for example, contrasted the printer's horizontal flatbed, in which slugs of letters are set, with the vertical canvas of easel painting. For Douglas Crimp the exploitation of a flatbed printing technique by artists like Rauschenberg

29

16 Walter Benjamin, 'Peinture et graphisme', *La Part de l'oeil*, no. 6 (1909), p. 13.
17 Rosalind Krauss, 'Horizontality', in *Formless: A User's Guide*, Yves-Alain Bois and Rosalind Krauss (Zone Books: 1997), pp. 93–4.

allowed the deterritorialization of painting from its historical identity as a discipline.[18] Here Benjamin's distinction of axis is combined with his thesis on art and mechanical reproduction.[19] The transversal is not simply the plane of signs in terms of the text but also the plane of machinic operation, inscription and reproduction. Clearly, it is the rotation of landscape onto the horizontal that is put on the table by Wall and many others.

This same dialectic of horizontality and verticality also operates in Deleuze and Guattari's *A Thousand Plateaus*. In this text, the vertical is aligned with the portrait. The face, or the mode of representation they call faciality, is a model to be copied, a picturesque machine to be replicated; difference is understood as deviance. It was not just Freud who argued that verticality is crucial to the essence of the human; humanism and culture have traditionally been aligned with verticality, especially in phenomenology and cognitive science. Being human – that is, being a humanist subject – is to be identified, portrayed, on the vertical axis. We might make this more general however and state that all identification – racial, gender, epistemological and ontological – occurs in the vertical mode of the portrait. The vertical is the axis of the model and the copy.

Moreover, in one of their rare explicit references to architecture, Deleuze and Guattari continue to define its praxis as the 'positions it ensembles – houses, towns or cities, monuments or factories – to function like faces in the landscape they transform'.[20] As with many of their observations on architecture, this is highly conventional; one recalls the Villa Savoye roofscape, in which a rectangular cutout 'frames' a view of the surrounding countryside into a 'landscape'. This is an architecture of discrete objects and isolated monuments. Nevertheless, we can see that this architecture is also the frame by which the landscape as deterritorialized longitudinal cut becomes conceptually 'rotated' into a pictorial landscape. Like Georges Bataille, who defines architecture as anthropomorphic per se, Deleuze and Guattari treat architecture as the model of faciality and verticality. Architecture is the model Oedipus, the mark of identity, the portrait of the 'same'.

However, Deleuze and Guattari argue, 'The face has a correlate of great importance: the landscape, which is not just a milieu but a deterritorialized world.'[21] If the vertical face is aligned with the humanist subject, then the horizontal landscape is the mode for all of their processes of anti-Oedipalization: the 'body without organs', the 'becoming animal', the

18 Rauschenberg famously printed text, images from art history, industry and various detritus onto a single surface. For Crimp, it is a heterotopia in the most literal sense, a landscape upon which the most incongruous elements exist in a coherent (but not whole) organization. Because they were removed from any context or grand narrative, the transversal can function as the site of simulacra, the site for the proliferation of copies without a designating Oedipal model. Douglas Crimp, 'On the Museum's Ruins', in *Postmodern Culture*, Hal Foster, ed. (Pluto Press: 1985). We might make an informative comparison between Boccioni and Rauschenberg. Boccioni's work remains within a tradition of easel painting and the pictographic. It remains literally and conceptually oriented along the vertical-longitudinal axis but attempts to articulate operations which occur upon the horizontal-transversal. On the other hand, Rauschenberg's combines and flatbeds are oriented along the transversal-horizontal but re-present longitudinal-vertical representations. The latter are transformed from pictures into informational signs that can be freely recombined. As Crimp argued, Rauschenberg's surfaces are archaeological sites in which representations and pictures are transformed into graphic and diagrammatic events defined by collision, superposition, blending, merging. Further, they employ the technology, concepts and techniques of media and mechanical reproduction to unfold new formal, spatial and aesthetic potentials. Like Pollock's *Deep Fathom Five* or Warhol's *Dance Diagrams*, Rauschenberg's work emerges from an encounter with painting as a discipline aligned on the vertical with the practices of the transversal. We might say they are not painted depictions of landscapes, either conceptual or pictorial, but events in which painting becomes or encounters the axis of transversal landscape.
19 It is important to differentiate the flatbed from collage. For no matter how similar they may appear, the cubist collage retains the 'longitudinal' mode in that disparate fragments are reassembled into a picture. In Rauschenberg's flatbeds, so it goes, something different is at stake: longitudinal representations are transformed into transversal marks, a type of *écriture*. Rauschenberg's flatbeds thus remain 'horizontal', that is, their mode is always transversal whatever their literal orientation.
20 Deleuze and Guattari, *A Thousand Plateaus* (Athlone Press: 1988), p. 172.
21 Deleuze and Guattari (1988), p. 172.

rhizome, nomadology, the war machine. In any case, landscape plays a central role in their project to 'reverse Platonism' by allowing simulacra – those things which have no model and which do not operate according to a logic of resemblance – to rise up against their masters, the model and the copy. These new simulacra can produce new subjectivities. Think of Kafka's machines in *In the Penal Colony*, or masochism, which Deleuze and Guattari examine as deterritorialization of the vertical body into a transversal site of intensity and desire, a body without organs. The masochist does not attack the body, they argue, but the Oedipalized image of the body, its vertical representation. But this is an extreme case. 'One need not literally deface the image of a body in order to attack the verticality of axis the body shares with culture: it was enough to attack the axis itself to undermine the two together', writes Krauss.[22] Through such a transversal mode, the subject is transformed into a landscape of difference rather than a portrait of identity. Could they also be productive of new subject matters?

This is in fact how Krauss reads the move towards the horizontal-transversal axis: as an undermining of the traditions of mimetic representation based on models, copies and truth. An art based on the horizontal-transversal is central to her and Yves-Alain Bois' reworking of Bataille's l'*informe*. In the otherwise heterogeneous examples of Pollock's *Deep Fathom Five* and Warhol's *Piss Painting*, Krauss detects a singular transversal modality. For Krauss, the rotation of the 'image from the axis of the vertical and into the horizontal' is a 'powerful weapon' against the gestalt and the Oedipalization of humanist representations.[23] Similarly against architecture, Deleuze and Guattari see the potential of painting as 'the deterritorialization of faces and landscapes, either by a reactivation of corporeality, or by the liberation of lines or colours, or both at the same time'.[24]

Remembering architecture's investment in the unified body as model, and upon which the city as a designed object and object of design knowledge was supposedly modelled, we might propose that its recent encounter with landscape design is not unlike a masochism which operates at the level of the discipline. A masochism upon a 'body of knowledge'. Through landscape, architecture attempts to transform its body-model and its status as a model, to deterritorialize its own representation and self-image into a landscape upon which new intensities might be unfolded and desires discovered. Architecture and urbanism would then not simply fashion landscapelike plans or pay formalist homage to 'bodies without

22 Krauss (1997), p. 103.
23 Krauss (1997), p. 103. For this reason, Greenberg insists that only when Pollock's paintings are rotated onto the vertical surface of the gallery wall are they recuperated into the tradition of painting. Before that they are 'base material' rather than 'art'.
24 Deleuze and Guattari (1988), p. 172.

organs' but begin to operate and intervene according to a transversal mode. Moreover, if mechanical reproduction and graphic concepts were central to the advent of transversal paintings, the use of digital visualization and information technology in landscape urbanism should be understood as similar transversal operations in design, ones that may perhaps no longer be limited to these two axes and instead suggest as yet untheorized – that is to say, yet-to-be-pictured – modes of operation. Landscape cannot offer a new model of urbanism or architecture, only a new mode of operation. The proposition of landscape urbanism thereby attempts to rotate architecture out of its vertical alignment as a model of order, to deterritorialize in the first instance not the physical space of the city but the discipline's precepts and ethos. We might then say that the transdisciplinary project of landscape urbanism is an attempt to displace the traditional ethics of architecture based on the model-copy and to cultivate an architectural ethics of simulacrum.[25]

25 Architecture as simulation had been proposed previously by Peter Eisenman, in 'The End of the Classical', though in that piece the simulacra retain a negative connotation. Indeed, it is interesting to note that Bataille's *l'informe* emerged in architecture ten years ago, with Eisenman and Greg Lynn's attempt to develop an architecture of 'writing' that would displace representation and projective geometry with inscriptions of traces, indices, forces. In the wake of this project – which was largely abandoned before its accomplishment – architecture has adopted a projective rather than critical rhetoric. One reason landscape is useful is that its problematically pictorial overtones prevent the creeping realism, mimesis and objectivism that characterizes much of this discourse.

Lawrence Barth

Diagram, Dispersal, Region

Urban plans pose a simple question, the answer to which resists being settled: what is the city? The question inheres in the lines, colours and text of the plan, remaining unanswered even after the planners have satisfied themselves that their job is done. The question is not a local one; it does not ask after the fate of this city, but leads towards the potentials and possibilities of the urban. The question posed is the more strategic one through which a field of dispute is opened. It indicates material elements that are plainly visible. It suggests certain relationships among elements, of the sort that carry a demonstrable plausibility. But it is not a record so much as an incitement. The plan is not the expression of a subject – it marks the occasion for thought rather than its distillation. Neither does the plan stand as the representation of knowledge, however much it is obliged to incorporate and display the strata of knowledge. Plans are of necessity diagrammatic rather than representational.

One might object to this characterization of the urban plan, for it seems to collapse the practice of urbanism back into its general conditions and, in so doing, deny the distinction between representational and diagrammatic practices. It would suggest that even the most moribund and fixed of masterplans cannot avoid being drawn into an engagement with the strategic question of the urban, nor maintain some direct and immediate connection to the object world it proposes. More alarmingly still, it would seem to portray as gratuitous the many recent efforts to develop the diagram as a promising technique in urbanism. However, the intention here is not to deny the distinction but to open up another field in which distinctions are recognized and gain significance. Architecture's pursuit of the diagram focuses largely upon its capacity to postpone or perturb the movement from drawing to building, while less attention is directed to the effects of the diagram upon a strategic field beyond that axis. What follows is a short sketch concerning the condition and practice of diagrammatic urbanism, one which attempts a crude description of the shape of this wider strategic domain. Ultimately, the aim is to discover a heightened political and analytical significance for diagrammatic architecture as it moves more aggressively onto the terrain of urbanism.

If there is today a sense that modernist planning has subjected the city to a certain paralysis, stifled its vibrancy under a blanket of control and division, we might nevertheless pose a set of questions whose aim would be an analytical refinement of this complaint. First, has the city's dynamism been suppressed? Of course, there is an unavoidable relativism in any answer, but it would be difficult to read either Rem Koolhaas's *Delirious New York* or Mike Davis's *Magical Urbanism* and conclude, either in the way that the city has projected itself or in its continuing performance, that the city is anything other than scintillating in its generation of complexity.[1] Perhaps it is a case of urban vitality promoting a culture of dynamism that is not easily satisfied (Simmel noticed this pattern nearly a century ago). Some will persist in replying that urban complexity endures only in spite of the best efforts of planners, and that the static, object-orientated quality of plans themselves reveals the planners' intentions. However, this would be to suggest that certain plans not only contain the instruction to be read as representation, but that the instruction is sufficient to isolate the plan from the broader strategic questions. The distinction between diagrammatic and representational practices would be found purely on the terrain of drawing, rather than amidst the more extended set of practices of which drawing is a part. Just such a view of the analytic of drawing has been nicely rejected by Stan Allen in his writings on notation.[2] We began by describing the urban condition as itself diagrammatic. On this view, the century-long persistence of a certain concern with the regulation of urban change is itself an aspect of the diagram. Instead of simply promoting or suppressing the pulse of the city, the discourse of urbanism, including its plans, has consistently problematized urban dynamism as it sought the adjustment and alignment of progress and stability according to a dispersed field of urban reasoning.

The issue brings us to a second question. How should we attempt to place and understand the graphic component of urbanism? Emblematic of a common approach to this question within the critique of modernist urbanism is Colin Rowe's juxtaposition, in the introduction to *Collage City*,[3] of Le Corbusier's Plan Voisin and a photograph of a public housing project in New

1 Rem Koolhaas, *Delirious New York: A Retroactive Manifesto for Manhattan* (Monacelli Press: 1994); Mike Davis, *Magical Urbanism: Latinos Reinvent the US City* (Verso: 2000).
2 Stan Allen, *Practice: Architecture, Technique, and Representation* (G+B Arts International: 2000), esp. pp. 3–32.
3 Colin Rowe and Fred Koetter, *Collage City* (MIT Press: 1978).

York. The angle of the views and the cropping of the images are assimilated; the reader is being invited to see the effectiveness of the plan in the pattern of the built, and the tragedy of the built in the Utopianism of the plan. The meaning of each image is pressed immediately towards the other along an axis in which the built follows the conceived. We might admit, along with Stan Allen, that architectural drawing 'carries a mimetic trace, a representational shadow, which is transposed … into the built artifact'. But, he quickly continues, 'To think of drawings as pictures cannot account for the instrumentality of architectural representation nor for its capacity to render abstract ideas concrete.'[4] Two points may be highlighted in Allen's position. The instrumentality of the graphic component in urbanism is not properly captured in terms of the built environment that 'follows', and abstraction is a key element in the effectiveness of urban plans.

Graphics present instruments that linger closely around thought; they are directed, along with thought, to address or respond to a field of problems. The graphic aspect of the plan links questions of form and spatial relations in a field of urban problematizations. The fact that plans are ineluctably graphic shows minimally that the diagnosis of the urban proceeds through spatialization. If the instrumentality of the plan can be placed here, upon the terrain of an urban diagnostics, then the importance of abstraction should be discovered here as well. Certainly, it provides a means of anticipating the virtuality and unpredictability of the built form, as is widely recognized by architects in an era when they are noticeably moved by the work of, say, Eisenman and Koolhaas. But more importantly for work within urbanism, abstraction permits the strategic consideration of generalized functions and relations. The virtue of this capacity on the terrain of urban dispute is twofold. On the one hand, it divorces diagnosis from the question of immediate interests, that game of advantage among polarized and immobile camps, and links it to the broader field of knowledge and professional competence by which the urban comes to be a reasoned and governable domain. Here, diagnosis enacts the engagement between strategic function and stratified knowledge that Foucault explored under the couplet power/knowledge. Secondly, it introduces the line by which the exemplary may be brought to bear upon the singular case. The question of the local decision is dispersed onto the wider field of urban reason, where it may be treated as a case. The plan as diagram mobilizes this field of repetition and differentiation, effectively making it

4 Allen (2000), p. 32.

possible to treat the urban as a specific kind of environment subject to certain inherent characteristics, forces or processes. The repeatability of these functions and relations indicates the strategic or broader political dimension of the urban, for the question of what should be done in a particular location cannot justly be answered by narrowing the focus to the specifics of site or place. Instead, the question is addressed through a displacement onto a lateral field of generalization, possibility and regularity.

In this account, the diagram has been placed so as to find its effectiveness on a field of dispute articulated with particular domains of power/knowledge. This accords well with Deleuze's account of the diagram as an abstract machine. 'It is defined by its informal functions and matter … a machine that is almost blind and mute, even though it makes others see and speak.'[5] Moreover, the diagram is transformational; it multiplies effects. However, an ambiguity arises at the moment in which diagrammatic architecture proposes itself as the means to press beyond the impasse of what we take to be, in our generalized pursuit of formal and spatial innovation, a paralysis of urban development. The question is not whether diagrammatic practice is more suited than representational practice to the generation of a novel urbanism, for we may agree that it is, but whether in this capacity its performance aligns itself with power or beyond it. Of course, the point here is not to make a snap judgement for or against practical innovation, but to clarify the terrain upon which it is to be evaluated or understood. The question of diagrammatic architecture's relationship to power can be reformulated as two issues. First, how is power being thought to work when we tell ourselves that the rationality of planning has suppressed the innate dynamism and complexity of the urban process? The second issue is more complex, and can only be crudely sketched here, but raises the question of a properly urban diagram operating as power or, better, as an art of government, and itself distinct from panopticism. The two issues come together in Michel de Certeau's *The Practice of Everyday Life*, in which the possibility of a distinctly urban power is halfheartedly raised as the broad-scale counterpart to panopticism. In this account, power is presumed to operate as an overrationalizing gaze and as suppression deployed over the space of the city, beyond which everyday life – a kind of fecundity of form and action – continues to escape.[6] An architecture sympathetic to this view would see, rather naively, every formal or spatial innovation as an affirmation of life in the face of power.

5 Gilles Deleuze, *Foucault* (University of Minnesota Press: 1988), p. 34.
6 Michel de Certeau, *The Practice of Everyday Life* (University of California Press: 1984). For a more detailed critique of de Certeau's book in relation to the work of Jean-François Lyotard, see Lawrence Barth, 'Immemorial Visibilities: Seeing the City's Difference', in *Environment and Planning A*, 1996, volume 28, pp. 471–93.

Leaving aside Foucault's rejection of the idea that panopticism can be deployed uniformly over a surface area as large as a city's, it is nonetheless clear that he imagined power as something far less clumsy than a suppression that fails to take hold. What gives power its force and agility is its capacity to take hold with the movement of the subject – power is present when we wish and when we know. The point of Foucault's analysis of the panopticon was not to derogate the prison, but to question how our individualization had become a practicable political goal. Foucault's ultimate dissatisfaction with how this question had been handled in *Discipline and Punish* is well known, and it gave rise to his subsequent lectures on governmental reason and the final volumes of his *History of Sexuality*. In these works he returned to a theme that had been present in his earlier archaeological work, namely the questioning of the conditions under which the subject takes itself to be a problem. *Discipline and Punish* highlights the tactical performance of a technology that subjects one to individualization and normalization, but leaves in the background the terrain of governmental reason upon which the subject would problematize itself in relation to broadly political goals. One can imagine *Discipline and Punish* being rewritten to foreground the question, 'Through what specific reasonings about the problems of the subject is the diagram of panopticism taken up in so many varied locations?' The diagram would then emerge more clearly as that which mobilizes a lateral field of governmental reason, and which at the same time generates the punctual tactics of function and spatiality in well-defined areas of knowledge and practice. This view places the diagram as an instrument or practice inherent in a more general condition whose existence and transformation it both serves and engenders. Additionally, the diagram would be understood as a practice that places the subject in question in two senses, both as the object of specific human sciences and as a subject with a capacity for moral or political action.

Clearly, the urban cannot be identified with that which cultivates our individuality through the techniques of discipline – it is a different diagram. One quickly recognizes the value for urbanism of Deleuze's exposition of Foucault's diagram, for it presents spatial and functional abstraction as both the key to the diagram's performance and the possibility of its transfer to the urban field. However, Deleuze and Foucault are quite clear that it is not function and spatialization in general that make up the diagram, but specific pure functions and spatializations that define the machine. What is perhaps more obvious in Foucault's chapter on panopticism is that these functions and spatializations are revealed through the genealogical work of analysis. The urban is not discipline on a larger scale, nor is it simply the context or 'objective conditions' within which the machine works its transformative potential. The machine works through the dispersed urban field: a specific set of problematizations, a specific diagram that has its own genealogy. It is a diagram that deploys its own expressions and visibilities, apparent to us when we proclaim, for example, the advent of the regional metropolis, or describe the functionality of a space of flows. Moreover, it is a diagram that deploys the practice of urbanism in pursuit of an intrinsic dynamism. If it is clear that the urban presents a machinic landscape still wanting analysis, it is equally clear that Foucault's work on governmental reason has opened a broad avenue of enquiry for just such an investigation. Paul Rabinow's *French Modern* presents a clear acceptance of the invitation, detailing the key lineaments of a modern urban diagram.[7] Rabinow's work traces a series of transformations around the turn of the twentieth century through which the urban diagram becomes dramatically reconfigured. There is the alteration of scale over which the urban is understood to operate, from the *cité* to the *agglomération*. There is the emergence of the urban conceived as a sociotechnical milieu, the rise of the importance of statistical probability in the conception of populations, the transformation of the human material upon which the urban is thought to act and of which it must take hold. The urban plan as diagram emerged upon this dispersed field of transformations, and helped to organize it.

One aim of this essay has been to place urban diagrams in dispersal, understood here in three senses. First, the meaning of the diagram is found neither in the drawing nor in the built environment, but in the extended process of which the drawing of plans is part. Secondly, this process is not well captured upon a single axis in which the plan leads inexorably to the built, however deferred or open to alteration, but in relation to a field of dispute around the building and governing of cities. Thirdly, because the plan acts as diagnosis, it also disperses onto a terrain in which the subject questions its capacity for action and difference. Dramatically dispersed in these ways, it is unsurprising that urbanism has found itself exceeding the scale of the city, loosened from the grasp of the municipality, attentive to the possibilities of speed and intrigued by the differential functional capacities of the abstract machine. Diagrammatic

7 Paul Rabinow, *French Modern: Norms and Forms of the Social Environment* (MIT Press: 1989).

practices within urbanism respond to these conditions, but not because they have only recently been thrust upon us. The regional metropolis is not that which has happened to the urban over the last three or four decades, but that which urbanism has been diagramming fairly consistently since around 1920. The practice of a diagrammatic urbanism presents an immanent response on a dispersed field that it helps to shape. Its aim cannot be simply the postponement of form, nor even the multiplication of forms and functions, but the challenge and interrogation of the urban diagram itself, both as a condition and as a practice.

MEDIUM ▸

In its renewed framework, the proposition of urban responses involves the simultaneous constitution of a medium that consistently generates those responses out of a multitude of stimuli. Through the management of multiscalarity, transpecificity, prephysicality, intensivity and virtuality, such a medium intends to overcome operatively the persistence of five distinctive problems in urbanism: the difficulty in transposing information across scales, the need to move across realms of specificity and expertise, the engagement with the multiple forces that operate before the physical, the control of transformations through anticipation, and the regulation of temporal processes through direct determination. Landscape urbanism permeates segregated domains by installing itself before them through the construction of a machinic medium. Abstract without being reductive, virtual without being ideal and ubiquitous without being Utopian, the machinic is a technically controlled sieve that acquires consistency as it integrates a multiplicity of determinations in a medium of production, virtualizing potentials by constantly oscillating between management of information, programming of responses, generation of organizations, evaluation of performance, coordination of collaborations, scripting of protocols, coding of communication, engineering of materials, modulation of expression and fine-tuning of inflections.–CN

Sedimentation

The physical conditions in the fabric are reduced to a system capable of receiving non-physical determinations through variations in its configuration. Determinations are categorized as informational inputs, then quantified and sedimented in the organization as they are associated one by one to simple parameters of variation in the geometry. A single matrix indexes them in the organization of the river edge.

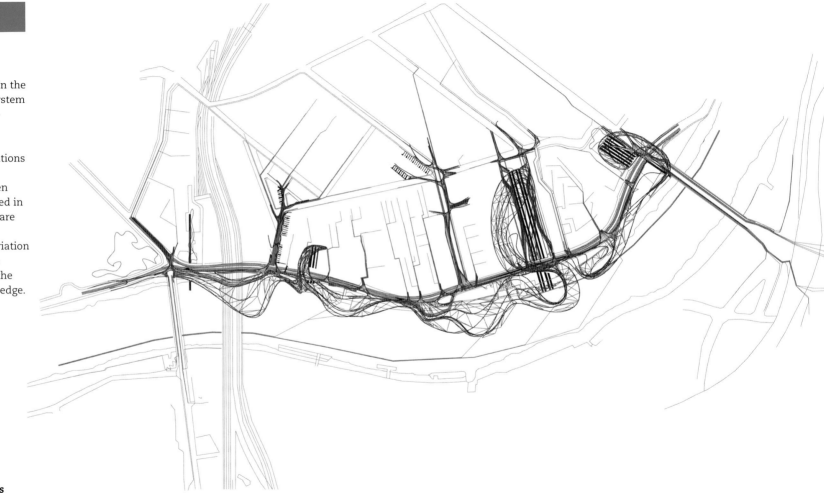

Roxana Scorcelli
Urban Excess/River Access

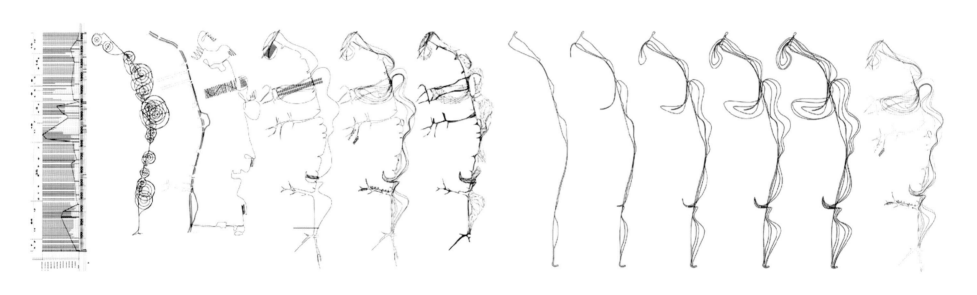

Permeation

Fragmentation, availability, use and value of land are used as gradients of resistance to the permeation of public corridors. The gradual slackening of local regulations and property rights allows their lateral expansion. As paths expand, linear subsystems of recreation erode the fabric until it reaches its ultimate fragmented configuration.

Fabian Hecker
Emerging Public Spaces

Permeability

Plot availability

Fragmentation and value

Potentials

Initial corridors

Intermingle

Two systems negotiate for space and intermingle their modalities. A regular plantation network loosens the links between individuals. A regular circulatory loop curves locally. The two systems adjust to each other within very tight limits: maximum distance in one case and maximum segmentation in the other. This triggers a mutual repositioning to avoid each other's restrictions while taking advantage of each other's flexibility.

Reciprocity

A loop is segmented as a way of filtering information along its longitudinal direction. The system restricts the sensitivity of each of its sections with the variations of those immediately around it. It acquires a self-controlled inertia based on reciprocity.

Frven Lim
Loop/Pool

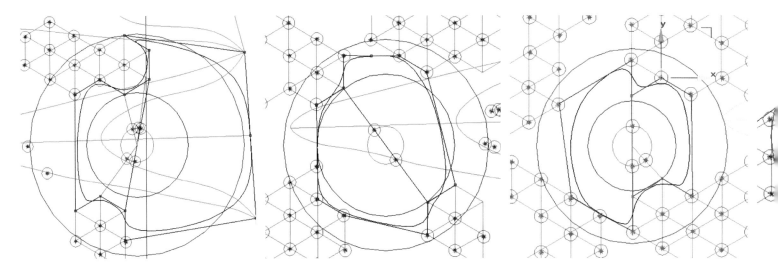

Loop-trees/accommodation

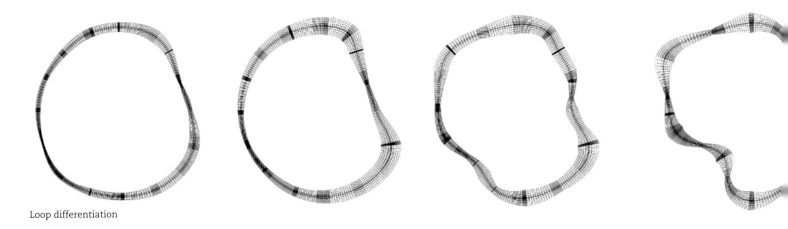

Loop differentiation

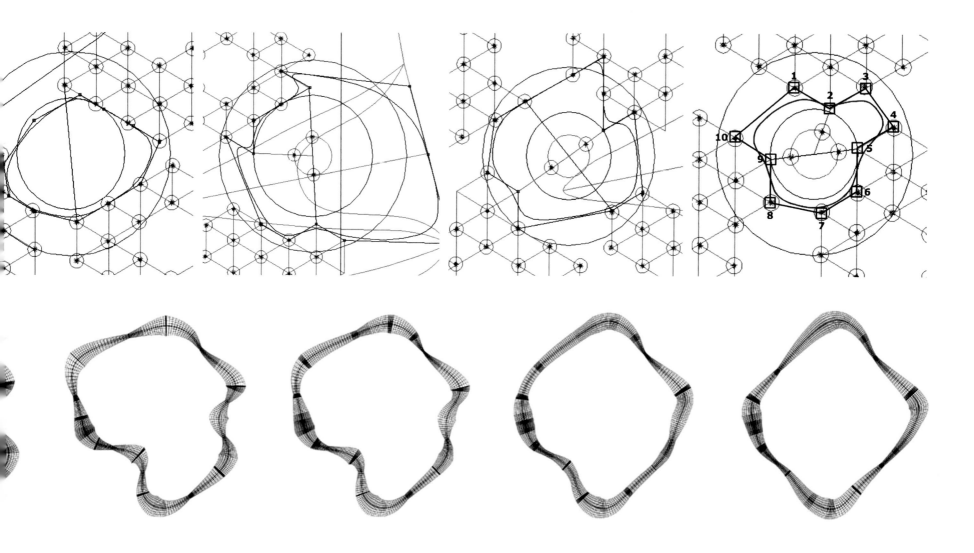

Templates

Ground, structure and walls are are laterally unfolded. The circulatory loops are dissected to allow the measurement and evaluation of relative surface areas, structural rhythms and variation of curvature in the continuity of the surface.

Equalizing

Circulation is measured across a field and transposed into a field of repelling forces. Intensity activates rugosity and distributes piles of earth on the new ground. This gradient is pixelated according to five generic sizes, which correspond to equal organizational scales. While provisionally segregated, the multiplicity is integrated in a common modularity. The equalizing system regulates intensities, manages hierarchies and finetunes the degree to which each scale affects the final organization.

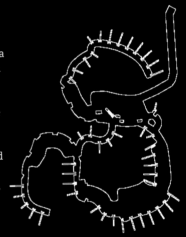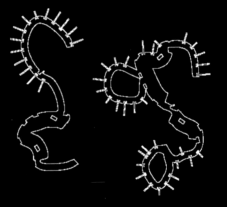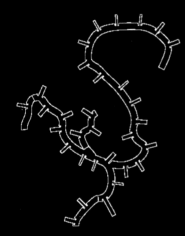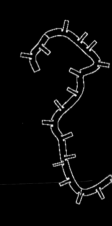

Frven Lim
Loop/Pool

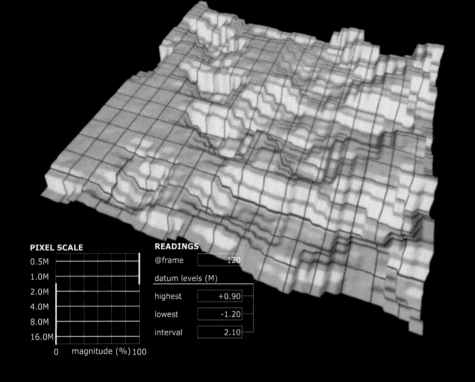

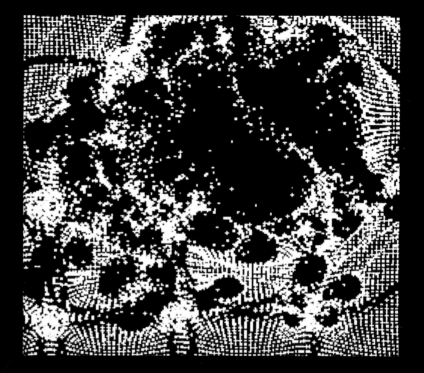

Vectorial Scanning

Topography and infrastructure are integrated in a system of dynamic scanning. Several speeds of circulation evaluate the visual continuity of the territory from the point of view of the car's driver. A regulation of cones of vision and limits of speed (their rhythms, gradients and leaps) carves the land, creates programmatic envelopes, adjusts the curvature of the road system and instructs the distribution of switches and interchanges.

Jose Parral
Artland

TOPOGRAPHY

Field intensities are graded for the placement of art and topograpic framing.

VISUAL FIELD GRADATION

8 7 6 5 4 3 2

FULL TOPOGRAPHIC
DEVELOPMENT
NORTH SECTOR

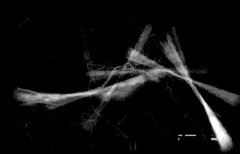

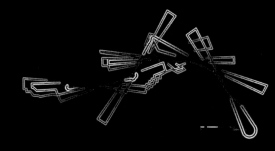

SPEED 50 MPH HIGHWAY

SPEED 50 TRAJECTORY

SPEED 50 VISUAL FIELD

SPEED 50 TOPOGRAPHY

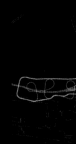

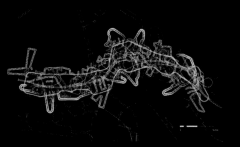

SPEED 30 MPH HIGHWAY

SPEED 30 TRAJECTORY

SPEED 30 VISUAL FIELD

SPEED 30 TOPOGRAPHY

TOPOGRAPHY

Field intensities are graded for the placement of art
and topograpic framing.

VISUAL FIELD GRADATION

8   7   6   5   4   3   2   1

FULL TOPOGRAPHIC
DEVELOPMENT
NORTH SECTOR

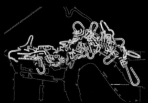

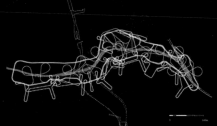

SPEED 15 MPH CRUISE LOOP

SPEED 15 TRAJECTORY

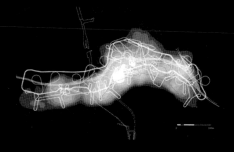

SPEED 15 VISUAL FIELD

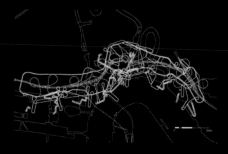

SPEED 15 TOPOGRAPHY

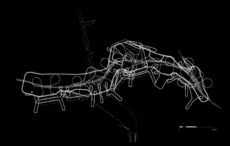

SPEED 5 + 0 MPH PARKING

SPEED 5+0 TRAJECTORY

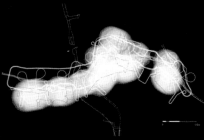

SPEED 5+0 VISUAL FIELD

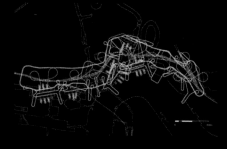

SPEED 5+0 TOPOGRAPHY

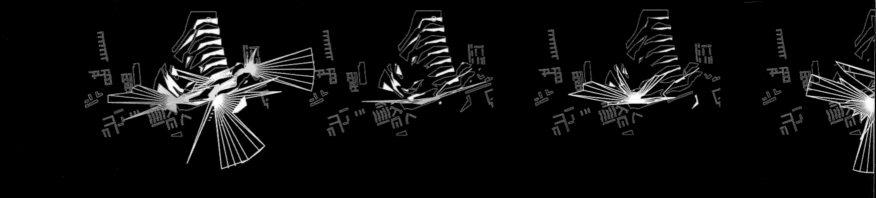

Julian Varas
Inhabiting the Artificial Ground

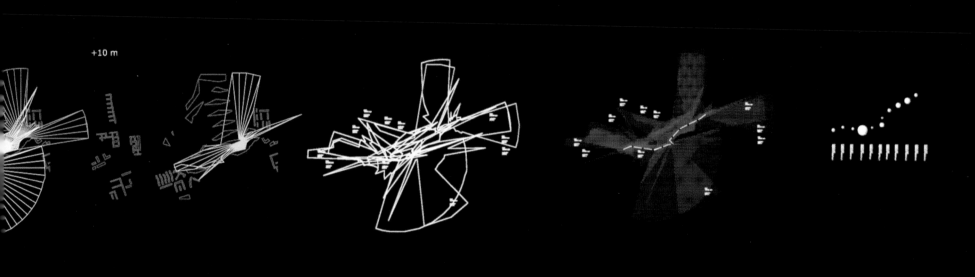

+10 m

Journey Through the Picturesque (a Notebook)

52

And why should our hope be in vain? We believe that landscape painting should one day shoot hitherto unknown sparks, when the great artists cross the frontiers of the Mediterranean more often and penetrate further from the coast, when they are able to embrace the immense variety of nature in the humid valleys of the tropics, with the native freshness of a pure, young soul.

ALEXANDER VON HUMBOLDT, 1847

Puppy communicates love, warmth and happiness to everyone. I created a contemporary Sacred Heart of Jesus.

JEFF KOONS, 1992

The side of the smooth green hill, torn by floods, may at first very properly be called deformed; and by the same principle, though not with the same impression, as a gash on a living animal. When the rawness of such a gash in the ground is softened, and in part concealed and ornamented by the effects of time, and the progress of vegetation, deformity by this natural process, is converted into picturesqueness; and this is the case with quarries, gravel pits, etc., which at first are deformities, and which in their most picturesque state, are often considered as such by a levelling improver.

UVEDALE PRICE, 1810

The effect of such a marsh in the city would be novel, certainly, in laboured urban grounds, and there may be a momentary question of its dignity and appropriateness ... but [it] is a direct development of the original conditions of the locality in adaptation to the needs of a dense community. So regarded, it will be found to be, in the artistic sense of the word, natural, and possibly to suggest a modest poetic sentiment more appreciated by town-weary mind than an elaborate and elegant formal garden would have been.

FREDERICK LAW OLMSTED, 1882

Our green is dark, almost black, and by strange contrast it is allied to two dominant colours: the yellow acacias and lapachos, which make the chromatic composition vibrant, and the purple cuaresmas, as if they were made to create the ritual atmosphere of Easter. Nature presents these unique colours together, making them compete against the pink tones of the palo-borrachos to provide the right measure in the composition. We also find an 'allegro vivace' in the shape and rhythm of the mountains which contrasts with moments of contemplation, the 'adagio' of the valleys and plains.

ROBERTO BURLE-MARX, 1942

And do you know what 'the world' is to me? Shall I show it to you in my mirror? This world: a monster of energy, without beginning, without end;... enclosed by 'nothingness' as by a boundary; not something blurry or wasted, not something endlessly extended, but set in a definite space as a definite force, and not a space that might be 'empty' here or there, but rather as force throughout, as a play of forces and waves of forces, at the same time one and many, increasing here, and at the same time decreasing there; a sea of forces flowing and rushing together, eternally changing, eternally flooding back, with tremendous years of recurrence, with an ebb and flow of its forms; out of the simplest forms striving towards the most complex, out of the stillest, most rigid, coldest forms towards the hottest, most turbulent, most self-contradictory, and then again returning home to the simple out of this abundance, out of the play of contradictions back to the joy of concord, still affirming itself in this uniformity of its courses and its years, blessing itself as that which must return eternally, as a becoming that knows no satiety, no disgust, no weariness: this, my Dionysian world of the eternally self-creating, the eternally self-destroying, this mystery world of the twofold voluptuous delight, my 'beyond good and evil', without goal, unless the joy of the circle is itself a goal; without will, unless a ring feels good will towards itself.

FRIEDRICH NIETZSCHE, 1888

i want to be a machine.

ANDY WARHOL, 1970

Les hommes ont voyagés, les plantes avec. De ce brassage immense confrontant les fleurs de continent depuis longtemps séparés, naissent des paysages nouveaux. Les plantes échappés des jardins raisonnés n'attendent qu'un solo à leur convenance pour s'épanouir. Le vent, les animaux, les machines transportent les graines aussi loin que possible. La nature utilise tous les vecteurs capables d'entremise. Et dans ce jeu des mariages, l'homme est son meilleur atout. Le jeu des transformations bouleverse constamment le dessin du jardin. Tout est entre les mains du jardinier. C'est lui le concepteur. Le mouvement est son outil, l'herbe sa manière, la vie sa connaissance.

GILLES CLÉMENT, 1994[1]

Processes of heavy construction have a devastating kind of primordial grandeur. To organize this mess of corrosion into patterns, grids and subdivisions is an aesthetic process that has scarcely been touched.

    Art can become a resource that mediates between the ecologist and the industrialist. Ecology and industry are not one-way streets, rather they should be crossroads. Art can help to provide the needed dialectic between them. I am convinced that the future is lost somewhere out in the trash heaps of the non-historic past.

ROBERT SMITHSON, 1968–70[9]

Perhaps the key issue is to do with designing emptiness, to decide where nothing will go. This word emptiness is enigmatic, has a sense of wonder and an almost inbuilt potential for getting one's imagination going and provoking involvement. I feel such an 'emptiness' is inherent to certain landscapes. It can also be found in cracks, or holes in the city, where there

1 [Men travel, and plants with them. From this great intermixing, this collision of flowers from long-parted continents, new landscapes are created. The plants in ordered gardens are simply waiting for the right moment to escape, to spread on their own. Wind, animals and machines carry seeds to the furthest corners. Nature employs all viable lines of intervention. And in her game of matchmaking, man is the key agent. Everything is in the hands of the gardener. He is the creator. His implement is movement, his method is greenery, his knowledge is life.]

54

cease to be rules, leaving the spaces to grow wild. Such places spark not only my imagination, but also the imaginations of people who come to inhabit them. Nonetheless, designing in these situations is a very delicate thing because such wildness is so fragile and can all too easily be destroyed. Even a successful intervention can only briefly sustain a lawless environment. The key is to do 'almost nothing', as Mies once said. I find this to be a very provocative statement and good starting point.

FLORIAN BEIGEL, 1997

Wasteland

The dissolution of the opposition between nature and artifice on every scale requires a programme of works that is nothing less than the rediscovery, through architecture, of the contemporary human position in the world. 'Areas of impunity' are precisely the zones where, as an exception, we find this ambiguous condition imprecisely defined as public or natural space. They are formerly degraded zones, endowed with a new urbanity by the gaze of new social subjects. Look at the wastelands beyond the outer suburbs, look at the way almost all the emerging forms of socialization have been constructed in them (although – or precisely because – they are deregulated territories). We are tempted to ask whether they might contain a metaphoric model, or whether it is possible to think of their complement, de-edification, given that the term 'wasteland' embodies a fascinating concept: land that has lost its attributes before the approach of the city, that is sterilized as the occupation proceeds, but also given a transcendental role in its new context. We ask ourselves whether architecture could be constructed in the same way.

Ecomonumentalism

We have got used to thinking of architecture in terms of place, believing it holds the key to our ability to tackle the project. Many forms of anchorage to the place have been developed in recent decades, from those involving the phenomenological root (*Anchoring* is the title of an important text by Steven Holl) to attitudes that arose at the Frankfurt School (Kenneth Frampton and his contextualism), via the Bergsonian influence in Moneo's work and the structuralist effect of the 'genius loci' in Aldo Rossi. In recent years we have witnessed an important shift: every location has begun to be regarded as a landscape, either natural or artificial, and has ceased to be a neutral backdrop, more or less decidedly sculptural, for architectural objects. With this change in point of view, the landscape becomes the subject of possible transformations; no longer inert, it can be designed, made artificial. The landscape has become the primary interest, the focal point of the architect.

At the same time, architecture is increasingly acknowledging the forms and conditions of nature in its composition and construction. This inclination towards environmental sensitivity and formal complexity is a response to new values in our society. The project is validated insofar as it constructs a complete redescription of the place, proposing the invention of a topography. This dual movement from nature to the project and from the project to nature has resuscitated an 'ecomonumental' condition that is beginning to push inexorably beyond the argument of opportunity in a way that some would say reflects the spirit of the time.

Hybrid Technique, Crossbred Style

Sensitivity towards nature-orientated policies has influenced technical paradigms, with interest shifting from high-tech experiments – no doubt a residue of the modern spirit – towards hybrid models in which the accent is placed on the interaction between natural and artificial materials. The former are massive and inert while the latter are light and energetically active, responding sensitively to environmental variations. This interaction is giving rise to composite systems in which natural materials are responsible for accumulating and reducing exchanges, while artificial materials act as generators, capturing energy resources.

This new technological model implies a shift from the aspects of material organization – exemplified by mass production, simplified assembly, time and cost optimization – towards the rational organization of the energy consumed during both the production and the upkeep of the building. This shift now enables us to conceive 'systems' not from the perspective of material congruence and unity, but rather in terms of environmental congruence, thus opening the way to experiments in which the congruous mixture of heterogeneous materials becomes a new visual feature. This hybrid materialism implies a profound transformation of aesthetic ideas in harmony with the crossbreeding of our designed landscapes.

Paradoxical conclusion: a new naturalism with no natural references. How did the colloquial use of 'natural' arise? 'Natural' or 'naturally' probably could not have been used in their present sense until nature was domesticated, understood, subjected to taxonomic organizations that gave a reasonable explanation for something previously construed as an inscrutable, threatening force. Nature first had to be contemplated as worthy of representation; a picturesque concept had to be superimposed on a certain degree of cosmogenic organization, the result of multiple journeys that provided the necessary distance and scope for observation. This is a plausible hypothesis that needs no ratification. Its mere mention allows us to imagine a new naturalism arising from the profound ambiguity in which nature is presented as the subject of knowledge and aesthetic experience: a hybrid, crossbred, entropic, humanized conglomerate that is confused with its former enemy – artifice – tightly wound into the political space, a carbon copy of what was once public space, a turbulent, flowing, random magma. Perhaps the key to the illumination of this expanding naturalistic gaze is to be found in the journeys yet to be taken, the dark zones of the atlas of the picturesque, those constant continents unconnected to the set of routes that hold it together. A new naturalism should begin by integrating these zones, bringing them to life and giving them a voice, demanding architectures that can be as meaningful in Lagos and Quito as they are in New York or Düsseldorf, architectures capable of articulating an immediate, unified sense of beauty, that could never be considered insulting or arrogant. Who can claim to have achieved such a thing today? But perhaps this fruitful journey can only be taken in reverse, from those dark holes towards ourselves, now reincarnated in the new indigenous peoples of a different form of wild nature. These journeys may well have begun already, though we – now the objects and not the subjects of a turbulent beauty to come – are as yet incapable of understanding them.

James Corner

Landscape Urbanism

Landscape urbanism brings together two previously unrelated terms to suggest a new hybrid discipline. Not unlike the combination of biology and technology to spawn biotech, or of evolutionary science with business management to produce organizational dynamics, the merging of landscape with urbanism suggests an exciting new field of possibilities. Such possibilities range from vistas across a new high-tech eco-metropolis – 'green cities' coloured by vegetated roofs and working gardens, and sustained by solar panels, wind turbines and stormwater wetlands – to those of a more postindustrial 'meta-urbanism', replete with brutalist layers of concrete intersections flying over densely packed houses, distribution centres and parking structures, collectively a 'landscape' by virtue of its flattened accumulation of programmes, textures and flows. Contradictory perhaps, but definitions and examples of landscape urbanism may be drawn from the regionally scaled and carefully planned ecological greenways of Stuttgart to the tough, unplanned, market-driven 'sprawl' of Los Angeles; from the exquisitely designed public spaces and streets of Barcelona to the densely layered unregulated spaces of Tokyo; from the infrastructural landscapes of roads, utility networks and hydrological systems of Phoenix to the symbolic representation of local identity undergirding cities as divergent as Las Vegas and Berlin; and from the reclamation of huge tracts of postindustrial land for new uses in Philadelphia to the planned erasure of underpopulated sectors of the city of Detroit. Each of these instances is valid and not necessarily exclusive of any of the others. Paradoxical and complex, landscape urbanism involves understanding the full mix of ingredients that comprise a rich urban ecology.

As a complex amalgam, landscape urbanism is more than a singular image or style: it is an ethos, an attitude, a way of thinking and acting. In many ways it can be seen as a response to the failure of traditional urban design and planning to operate effectively in the contemporary city. The complexity of market-based real-estate, community activism, environmental issues and short-term political mindsets has made it all but impossible for the urban planner to do much more than facilitate commercial development plans. With a lighter touch, greater ambition and more entrepreneurial techniques, landscape urbanism offers alternative approaches to urban practice. It marks a dissolution of old dualities such as nature-culture, and it dismantles classical notions of hierarchy, boundary and centre. Perhaps most importantly, it marks a productive attitude towards indeterminacy, open-endedness, intermixing and cross-disciplinarity. Unlike the overly simplified view of the city as a static composition, with the planner as the figure in charge, landscape urbanism views the emergent metropolis as a thick, living mat of accumulated patches and layered systems, with no singular authority or control. Such a dynamic, open-ended matrix can never be operated upon with any certainty as to outcome and effect. It escapes design and, even more so, planning. The contemporary metropolis is out of control – and this is not a weakness but its strength.

In viewing the city as a living ecology, landscape urbanism offers neither remedies nor fixes. Instead its protagonists look for opportunities to simply engage the dynamics of the city on their own terms, to be a player, an agent continually looking for ways to make a difference. But beyond opportunism, a propensity for cross-disciplinarity and an acceptance of – perhaps even a lust for – indeterminacy, what are some of the main characteristics of landscape urbanism as a practice? Here we can chart out five general themes:

1. Horizontality

Many social and cultural theorists have described the perceived shift of social structures from vertical to horizontal during the latter part of the twentieth century. Global economies, television, communication, mass-mobility and the increased autonomy of the individual are some of the factors undergirding a general transition from hierarchical, centric, authoritative organizations to polycentric, interconnected, expansive ones. A view across a city like Los Angeles makes this horizontal spread more palpable, animated by endless circuitries of movement and flow. From a landscape urbanist perspective, the emphasis now shifts from the one to the many, from objects to fields, from singularities to open-ended networks.

Horizontality maximizes opportunities for roaming, connecting, interrelating, assembling and moving – all while allowing differences to comingle and proliferate. And so the structuring of the horizontal surface becomes a predominant concern for landscape urbanism, for the surface is the organizational substrate that collects, distributes and condenses all the forces operating upon it. Land division, allocation, demarcation and the construction of surfaces constitute the first act in staking out ground; the second is to establish services and pathways across the surface to support future programmes; and the third is ensuring sufficient permeability to allow for future permutation, affiliation and adaptation. These surface strategies permit the creation of more or less coherent fields that allow an almost infinite range of varied and flexible arrangements. As vast organizing fields that establish new conditions for future development, these horizontal matrices function as infrastructures.

2. Infrastructures

Landscape urbanism implants new potential in a given field through the orchestration of infrastructural catalysts – infrastructures that perform and produce, or 'exfoliate' effects. In traditional landscape terms, such infrastructures might include earthwork grading, drainage, soil cultivation, vegetation establishment techniques, land management and so on – the preparatory substrate that conditions ground for subsequent uses. In traditional urban planning terms, infrastructures might include roads, utilities, bridges, subways and airports – the hidden systems that not only support but also instigate development. Codes, regulations and policies may also form part of the infrastructural milieu, as may many of the hidden forces, directions and regimes that work to shape development over time. The attention paid to the dynamic structures and processes that engender future development distinguishes landscape urbanism from more object-based ideas such as 'cityscape', 'infrascape', 'green city' or any other such hybrid image that derives from an objectified notion of formal appearance. Landscape urbanism deploys geometry, materials and codes less to control composition or determine social programme than to liberate future sets of possibility – cultural as well as logistical. It is an art of staging. And as such, it is an art that is concerned with spatial form and geometry less for stylistic or semiotic modes of expression and more for the effects that those forms and materials produce.

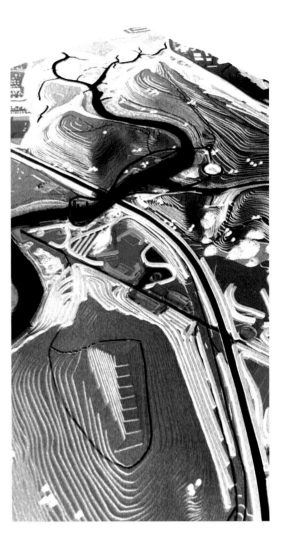

3. Forms of Process

In comparing modernist formal determinism to the more recent rise of communitarian 'new urbanism', the urban geographer David Harvey suggests that both these projects fail because of their presumption that spatial order can somehow control history and process.[1] He argues that the struggle for designers and planners ought to lie less with finding new spatial forms and aesthetic appearances than with 'the advancement of a more socially just, politically emancipating and ecologically sane mix of spatiotemporal production processes', challenging the general acquiescence to the forces of 'uncontrolled capital accumulation, backed by class-privilege and gross inequalities of political-economic power'. His point is that the processes of urbanization (in terms of capital accumulation, deregulation, globalization, environmental protection, codes and regulations, market trends and so on) are much more significant for the shaping of urban relationships than are spatial forms per se. Consequently, he argues that the search for new organizing structures and cities ought to derive from a Utopia of process rather than a Utopia of form. Here, the emphasis shifts from what things look like to how they work and what they do.

Now this is not to say that form and physical properties are unimportant; such an assertion would wrongly render the physical arts inert. An argument for process ought to recognize the profound effects form, space and materials exercise upon the world. And yet an argument for process must also demand that physical form and material be valued not only for their aesthetic and qualitative aspects but also for their instrumental and productive effects. Thus, whereas practices of design and planning concerned with time and process are fundamentally material practices, landscape urbanism emphatically puts these materials to 'work'. This marks a clear pragmatic impulse, but less a generic, expedient pragmatism and more a tactical, insightful form of practice, both entrepreneurial and creative. This focus upon material agency demands equal concern for technique.

4. Techniques

Techniques of operation are crucial for the success of landscape urbanism in practice. Given the many social, economic and logistical difficulties surrounding large-scale projects today, practitioners must be quick and light on their feet. The art of rhetoric and persuasion is key, as

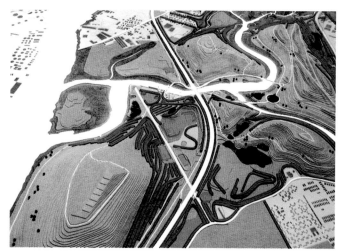

Freshkills, opposite and above

61

1 David Harvey, *Spaces of Capital: Towards a Critical Geography* (Routledge: 2001).

is the capacity to work with multidisciplinary teams and experts, but so too is a wily sense of dance, or play. A designer can no longer walk into meetings as heroic author or master-planner; one must be prepared to engage, converse, share, reflect and revise. Increasingly, projects today demand collaboration and interdisciplinarity, with architects, landscape architects, traffic engineers, ecologists, economists, artists and politicians all sitting around the table. While there is inevitably a tendency for such deliberations to stall through inertia, and to settle for the most familiar of common denominators (sameness), there is still the possibility of orchestrating a collective of experts and ideas towards a new synthesis. The art lies with the imagination and the capacity to lead – skills that are greatly enhanced through imaging and projection. Here, the pragmatic impulse might be cited again, for images are deployed not simply to 'sell' or 'get the job done' but more to query, explore, reorganize perceptions and synthesize different insights. Thus, the project may unfold in a truly inventive and unique way, 'getting the job done' but with new effects and consequences each time. Techniques drawn from landscape – such as mapping, cataloging, triangulating, surface modelling, implanting, managing, cultivating, phasing, layering and so on – may be combined with urbanist techniques – such as planning, diagramming, organizing, assembling, allotting, zoning, marketing and so on – to help create a larger bag of tools than the traditional planner has had in the past. Add to this Robert Rauschenberg's 'flatbed' procedures, John Cage's 'scorings', Buckminster Fuller's 'projections', or Michel de Certeau's 'micro-techniques' and you might just have the beginnings of a landscape urbanist's toolbox. Together, these sets of techniques service a new art of instrumentality, an art that may prove to be ever more relevant in the face of a world where cities will continue to see exponential population growth, increased environmental stresses, complex demands upon space, and radically weakened control and planning authorities.

In striving to comprehend these complex urban issues while also looking to achieve Harvey's 'advancement of a more socially just, politically emancipating and ecologically sane mix of spatiotemporal production processes' in a world gone awry, landscape urbanism offers some of the most compelling future directions. It can offer direction because of its extensive scale and scope, its inclusive pragmatism and creative techniques, its prioritization of infrastructure and process, its embrace of indeterminacy and open-endedness, and its vision of a more wholesome and heterogeneous world. Underlying all of these claims, of course, is the soft world of ecology.

5. Ecology

Ecology teaches us that all life is bound into dynamic and interrelated processes of codependency. Changes in the effects produced by an individual or ecosystem in one part of the planet can have significant effects somewhere else. Moreover, the complexity of these interactions escapes linear, mechanistic models or projections as layers of interrelationship create hidden cascades of effects to continually evolve forms in time. Such a dynamic, ongoing process of codependency and interaction is highlighted in ecology, accounting for a particular spatial form as merely a provisional state of matter on its way to becoming something else. In this sense, cities and infrastructures are just as 'ecological' as forests and rivers. This may be a hard point for traditional environmentalists to swallow, but the fact remains that everything is connected to everything else, and if the 'environment' is something always 'outside', then we fail to realize the full codependency and interactivity of things. Hence, we might speak of ecology as describing not a remote 'nature' but more integrative 'soft systems' – fluid, pliant, adaptive fields that are responsive and evolving. A soft system – whether wetland, city or economy – has the capacity to absorb, transform and exchange information with its surroundings. Its stability and robustness derive from its dynamics in its capacity to handle and process movement, difference and change. This is an attractive idea for landscape urbanism because it bears upon the continual need for cities and landscapes to be flexible, to be capable of responding quickly to changing needs and demands, while themselves projecting new sets of effect and potential. It also points to a revised activity in design practice: that is the active stirring of ecologies – eidetic and cultural as well as biological – in order to produce new combinatory mixes, new sets of effects, new transdisciplinary alliances and new kinds of public space.

A complex system is describable in terms of interconnected variables, such that for a variation in any variable there are changes in all those connected to it. Variables have a range within which the system performs with health and out of which it dies or, better, is forced to mutate. Within an upper and lower threshold of tolerance, a variable can move in order to achieve adaptation. When a variable adopts a value near its threshold, a system becomes uptight and loses flexibility. It is thus compelled to oscillate in order to disallow this uptightness, in a gymnastics of differentiation through which it learns and tunes itself. The understanding and simulation of urban organizations as complex systems dismantles the idea of the project as a closed object and enables the modulation of such flexibility through increasing approximation and rigorous adjustment. It also grounds interdependence between fields, and as a consequence it propagates potentials. The relationship between problems and solutions can thus be treated loosely, yet with precision, keeping differentiation open and complexification pliable. Rather than strategizing by decision-making, systemic simulation catalyzes tendencies, intensities, probabilities, feasibilities and impacts by iteration management. It abandons direct control and governs by loops.–CN

Breakdown

A manifold of woven
trajectories is dissected in
order to recognize nodes,
transversal segmentations
and longitudinal edges.
The dissection allows for the
evaluation of the system and
for the distribution of new
connective tissues.

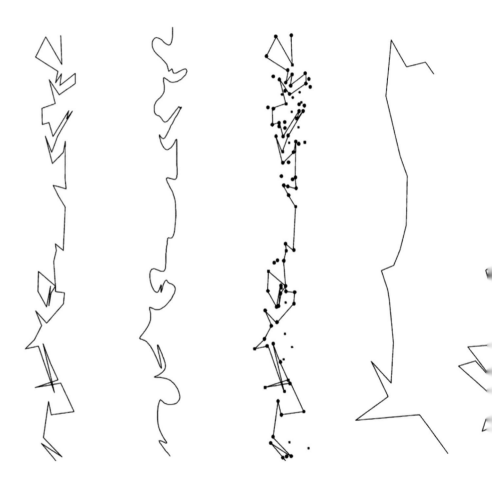

Roxana Scorcelli
Urban Excess/River Access

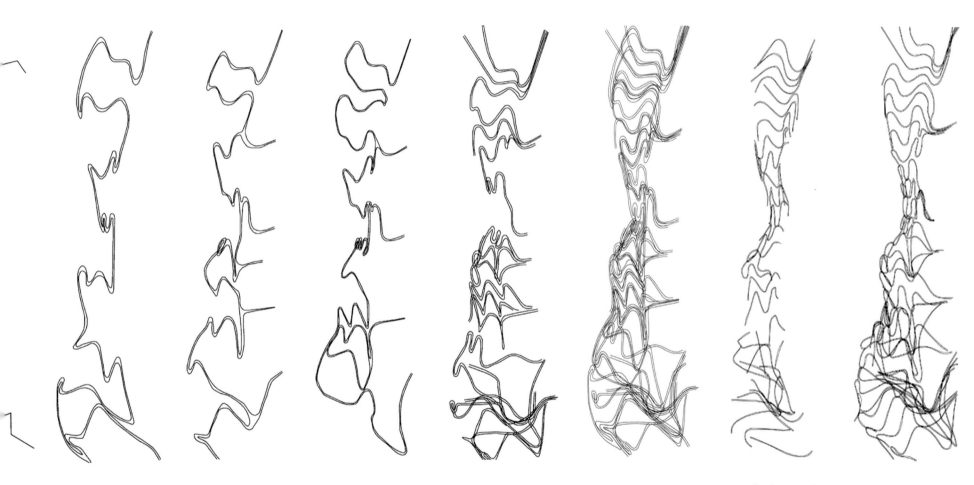

Circulatory and programmatic systems

Deviation

A repetitive system of
housing and local services
grows over abandoned areas
by deviation and configures
vortex-like communities,
where accessibility and
seclusion coexist.

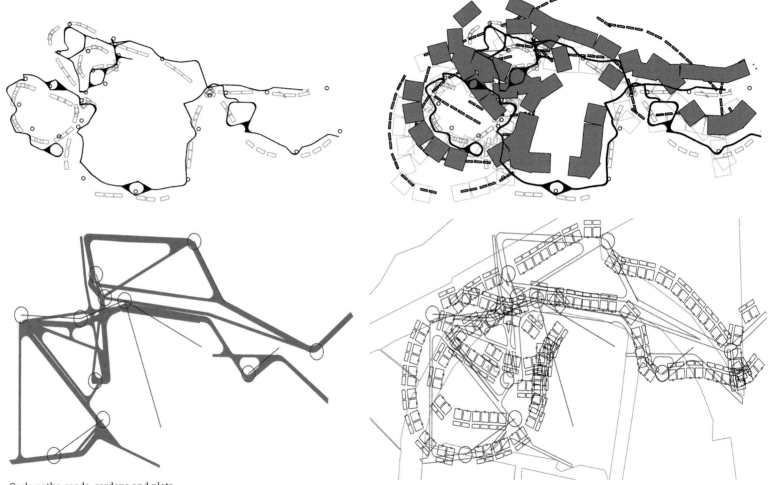

Nabeel Essa
The Un-Private Ground

Cycle paths, roads, gardens and plots

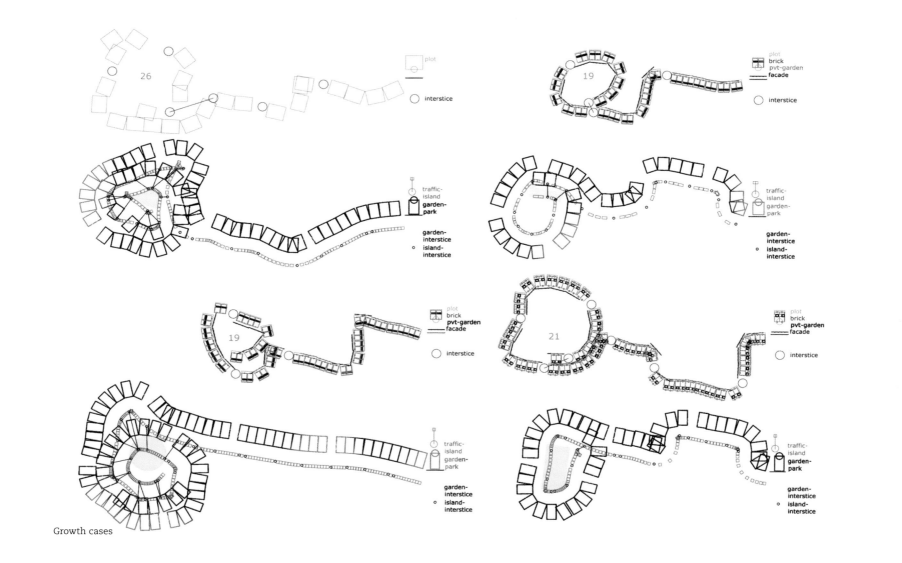

plot
brick
pvt-garden
facade

interstice

26

19

traffic-island
garden-park

garden-interstice
island-interstice

19

21

plot
brick
pvt-garden
facade

interstice

traffic-island
garden-park

garden-interstice
island-interstice

Growth cases

Layering

The differential curling of a
linear housing system interacts
with two modes of layering in
order to generate two types of
singularities. The first –
stacking units – allows the
management of growth
through the control of housing
densities. The second –
segregating services and
shared facilities – diversifies
the adaptation of the
organization at each stage
of its process of growth.

Nabeel Essa
The Un-Private Ground

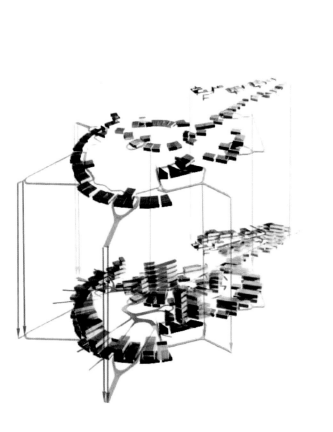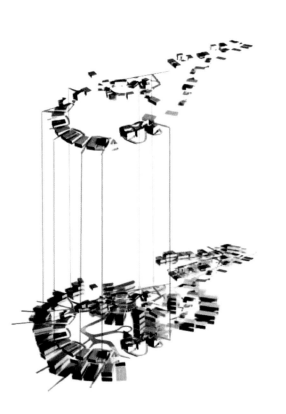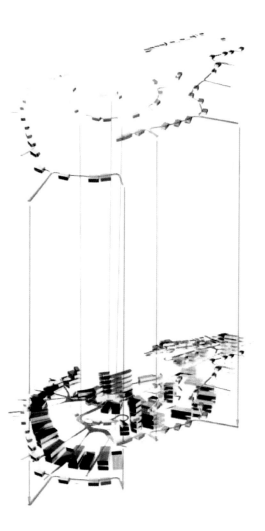

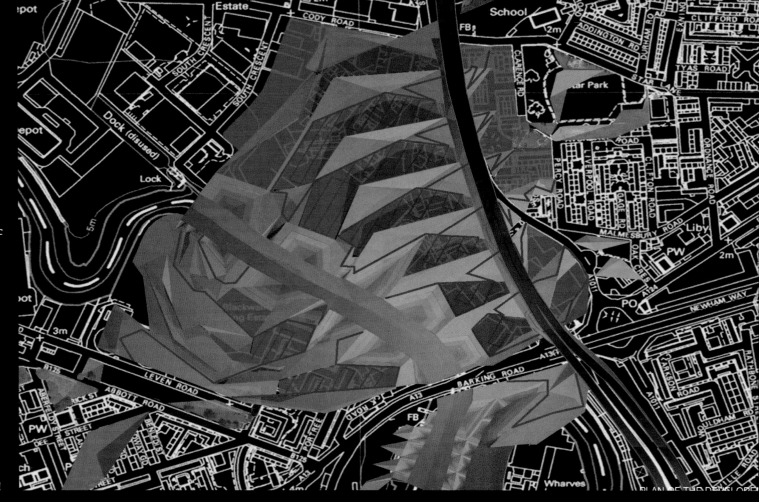

Triangulation

The horizontality of public space is textured and diversified through a system of triangulation that regulates built areas and integrates volumetric discreteness with superficial continuity.

Stratification

The horizontal sectioning of a maximum developmental envelope operates both as a tool for the quantification and evaluation of its programmatic potentials and as a device for its spatial striation.

Julian Varas
Inhabiting the Artificial Ground

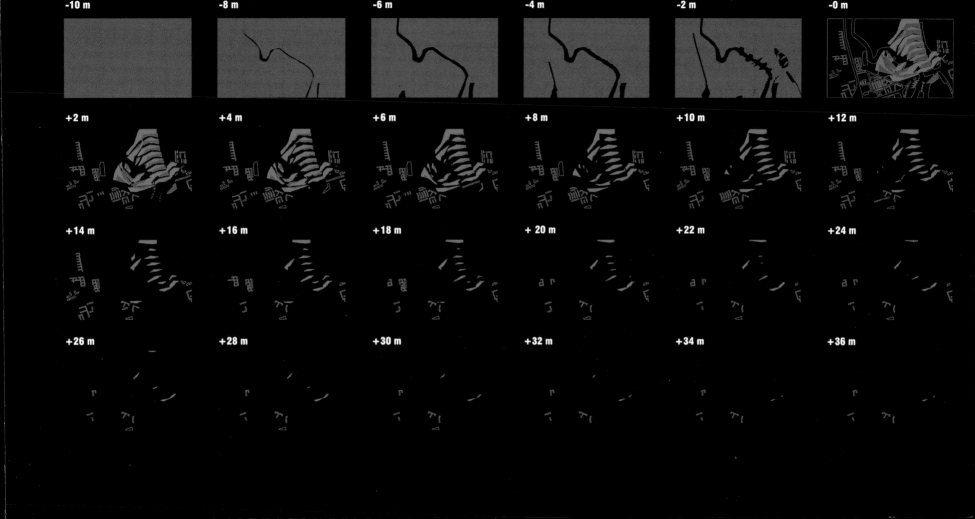

Transitions

The structural and circulatory merger between strands of circulation is solved by the incorporation of open zones, shared facilities and vertical connections. They operate as transitions in the intersecting areas and constitute points of orientation and transfer in the system.

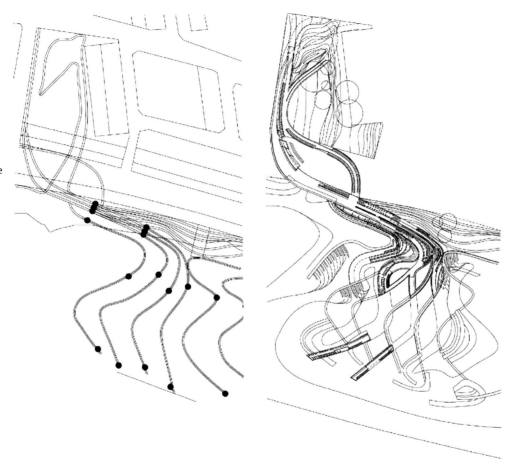

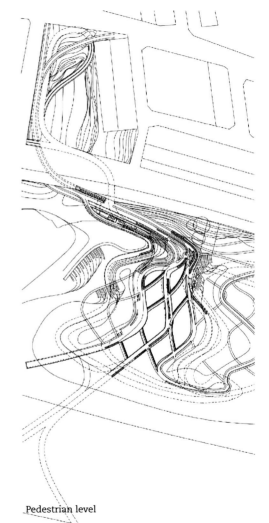

Roxana Scorcelli
Urban Excess/River Access

Infrastructure

Underwater level

Pedestrian level

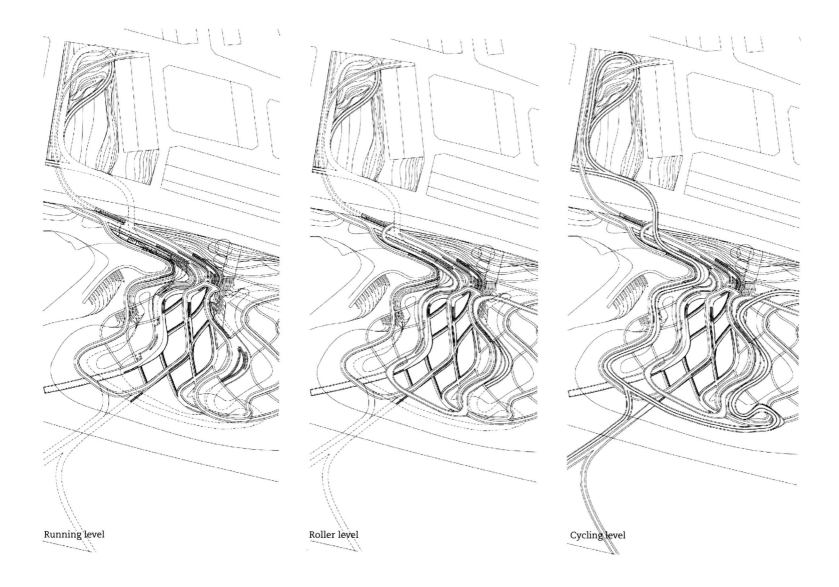

Running level

Roller level

Cycling level

Singularities

Areas of high-density or rapid variation, linear or centrifugal organization, diagonal continuity and intense roughness emerge as singular modes of collaboration between linear and triangulated systems running on a continuously faceted ground.

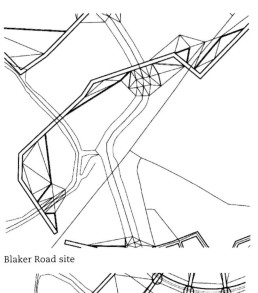

Blaker Road site

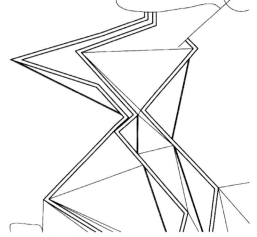

Stratford Rail lands

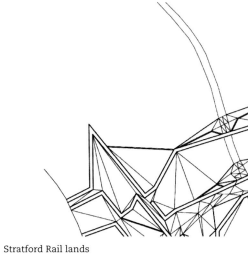

Stratford Rail lands

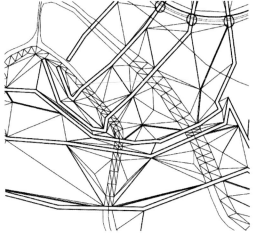

Thornton Fields

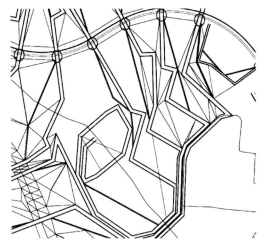

Carpenters Road site

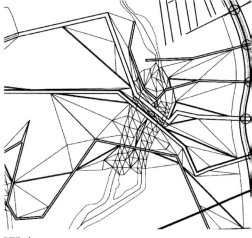

RTZ site

Julian Varas
Inhabiting the Artificial Ground

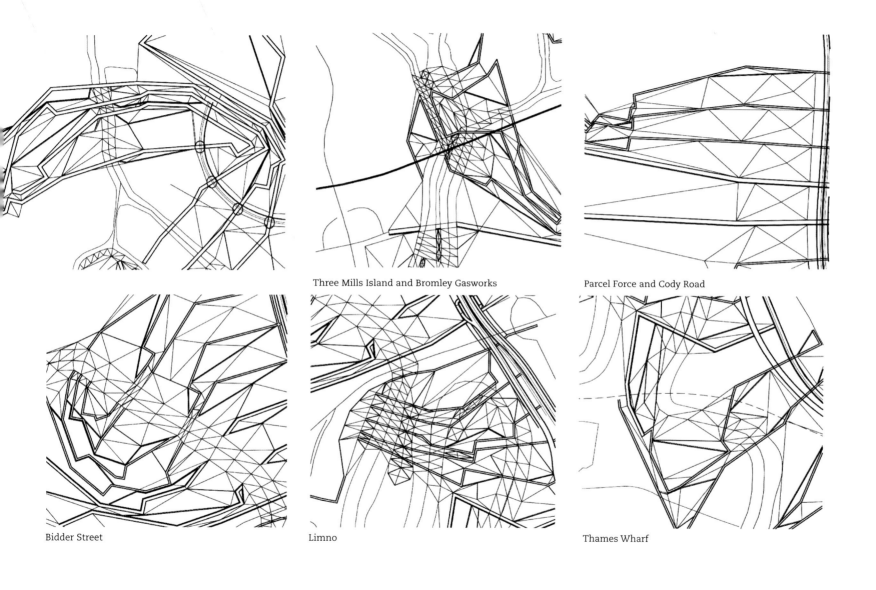

Three Mills Island and Bromley Gasworks

Parcel Force and Cody Road

Bidder Street

Limno

Thames Wharf

Florian Beigel & Philip Christou/Architecture Research Unit

Designing the Rug and Not the Picnic: Paju Landscape Script, Paju Book City, Seoul, Korea, 1999 – Present

Reading the Site

The long, broad valley of the Han River from the mountain in Paju to Seoul has a strong north-south linearity. When read from the horizon to the foot of the mountain – the guardian of Paju – the furthest lines or ribbons are the layered blue mountain ranges hugging the sky to the west of the river. Below is the band of the river's west bank. In the middle of the river are some discontinuous slithers, shifting slightly against each other, of sandbanks at low tide. Below this is the east bank of the river, a wide muddy shoreline. The elevated highway is signalled by the long dark band of its embankment in shadow, and by the rhythm of the very fine lighting masts. The low land of the Paju site between Paju Mountain and the Freedom Highway is structured by shorter dashes in the wetland, also in north-south formation, representing former flood-defence dams, delineating former rice fields.

The north-south linearity of the river landscape becomes the generator of the idea for Paju Book City as a built script in the landscape. Before developing this concept further, we have to read the recent history of the land by deciphering the traces of its gradual reclamation from the river. Paju Book City will be built on land reclaimed from the Han River. The Freedom Highway, connecting the site to the centre of Seoul and to the airport, and one day to North Korea, is built atop a ten-metre-high flood barrier along the east bank of the Han River.

The groundwater level of the reclaimed land is controlled by a fairly large drainage channel that meanders through it (see right), connecting an east-west array of little tributaries to the main drainage channel. This drainage system has generated a wetland with large areas of reeds, wild grass and watery expanses. Fishing activity indicates good water quality. Bird and insect life is well supported by this flora. In ecological terms, the site has biotopes of high value.

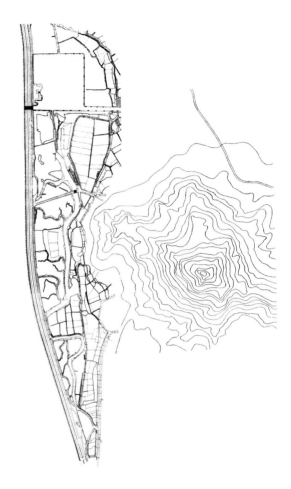

Time traces on the site at Paju, 1998 – small fields and drainage channels have been illegally constructed by farmers on the wetlands between the motorway and the mountain

Opposite: View of Paju from the mountain to the river, April 1999 (Philip Christou)

Territories of Coexistence

As designers of a new urban landscape, we feel we should tread carefully here. A strategy of territories of coexistence could be appropriate. We call it urban wetland. In more general terms, it is a city landscape. Paju Book City will be neither a city nor a built-up landscape: it will be both. In this way it will be a classic example of the contemporary urban condition. Returning to the view of Paju from the mountainside, we see, in the left-centre of the picture, two light-coloured patches. Alongside the larger patch, facing the mountain, are signboards inviting development. This is the landfill process in progress, providing plots of dry building land. Bringing in landfill material to raise the terrain above groundwater level is part of a standard civil engineering procedure, and the wetland habitat is now threatened. All the tributary drainage channels are to be filled.

Landscape Infrastructure

We are wondering whether the landfill strategy is selective enough. With the support of the Paju Association of Publishers, we have proposed a temporal and territorial reed infrastructure plan that remains in its original state or is cleared of landfill, based on the pattern of confluence of the land drainage system. This has gained limited acceptance by the central infrastructure development agency. This agency is also responsible for the design of Paju's transport infrastructure. The road pattern takes into consideration the military's need for unobstructed sightlines from the mountain to the river.

Urban Structures: Paju Landscape Script

The design is for phase 1 of the development, a 2100-metre-long site from the exit of the motorway in the south to the pumping station in the north. The urban plan consists of four long structures following the north-south landscape lines, as well as the urban solitaire of the distribution centre, which forms an artificial hill in the wetlands at the foot of the mountain and is the entrance to Paju from the motorway.

The main urban structures are: the printing factories in the shadow of the highway, forming a long chain of goods yards; the four-storey publishers' street, with a stratum of buildings that belongs to the street below the dyke of the highway and another stratum that

Sketch of mountain and wetlands, with large, sloping book-storage and distribution building (Florian Beigel)

Existing reeds, wetlands and mountain at Paju, February 1999 (Kim Jong Kyu)

78

belongs to the horizon and the view of the river landscape above the level of the dyke; the central spine of four-storey urban blocks with courtyards; and the street of four-storey live-work loft buildings, one side facing the channel and the other facing the mountain, dancing along the curvy lines of the site, the channel and the foot of the mountain.

'Sunken' into the wetlands at the south end, where the water channel meanders quite sharply, are irregularly curved stonelike buildings. The arrangement of east-west public voids (wetland corridors) connecting across the pattern of parallel lines facilitates river and mountain views. Together these structures could be seen as creating a texture within the existing landscape.

It is reminiscent of a 1928 etching by Paul Klee titled *Ein Blatt aus dem Städtebuch, 46 (N6)* (A Leaf from the Book of Cities). It is a scripture, a tabulation of city elements, similar to a textile, a texture. The plate for the etching appears to be a stone tablet. At the bottom of this tablet the title is inscribed and signed by Klee. The 'leaf' appears to be a parchment laid on this stone. The top third of the leaf has a kind of chapter *signum* that could be an abstracted sun with a strip of sky above and a horizon below. Below this is a text of pictograms consisting of an evolving city typology and continuing to the bottom of the leaf.

The pictograms are arranged in a series of horizontal lines sometimes attached, sometimes detached, and within the lines there are both attached and detached pictograms. There are basic patterns in the texture, with a high degree of repetition of form. Some lines consist of a row of basic types with variations. It is possible to associate building typologies with the pictograms. It is a sophisticated and rich composition.

This is an interesting representation of the city. It evokes a sense of a time before literacy and writing. A record of a civilization, or the city, is written down rather than made into a picture, as in a perspective description. This leaf is not a finite description of the city, because it is only one page out of a book, a fact signalled by the *46 (N6)* in the title. The painting somehow conveys an idea of a complex evenness and equality, like a group of characters. It also suggests a certain exchangeability and encapsulates a strong sense of relativity.

Designing a Building Within the Landscape Infrastructure

We are working on one of the publishing houses within the landscape infrastructure plan of

Urban structures, plan of landscape script, July 1999 (road layout predetermined by others):

(a) 'highway shadows' – grass-roof factories at height of the motorway (8 m);
(b) 'bookshelf units' – street buildings with courtyards (8 m), river-view buildings (7 m);
(c) 'spine units' – high-density buildings with courtyards (15 m);
(d) 'canal lofts' – oblique canal views and shallow-pitch roofs (less than 15 m);
(e) 'stepping stone' buildings in the wetlands;
(f) distribution centre – long, sloping artificial hill;
(g) 'urban island' – narrow lanes/atria and wetland gardens (15 m);
(h) canal/biotope territories with reed surface-water management system.

79

Paul Klee, *Ein Blatt aus dem Städtebuch, 46 (N6)*, 1928

Paju: the Youl Hwa Dang Publishing House, for the chairman of the Paju Association of Publishers. It must be an exemplary design, demonstrating the design principles of the 'bookshelf' type of building. We are collaborating with our former research fellow from the Architecture Research Unit, Kim Jong Kyu, who is now a distinguished architect in Seoul.

The essential building form emanates from the concept of a base building with patios in the lower world of the urban wetland and pavilions of the horizon on top. The base buildings belong to the publishers' street and to the workers' road to the rear, and the pavilions on top belong to the large landscape between Paju Mountain and the Han River.

The formal strategy for the ground building is to cut away from a solid prism. The cutout parts will be constructed with a polycarbonate and cast-glass wall. The outside, uncut perimeter walls will be made with a dark-stained timber rainscreen.

Architectural Infrastructures

Our urban landscape projects might be seen as a step towards understanding how architectural potential could be designed. It is not so much the completeness of an architectural artefact or proposal that is of interest here. The idea of the raw shell and its spatial condition continues to fascinate us. The words 'raw shell' have a wider meaning here, referring to structures of varying architectural scales that embody the essence, the implicit nature, of an architectural space. These we call architectural infrastructures. Besides their fundamental character, architectural infrastructures suggest unforeseen ideas for progressing the project. They are structures in which the past and the future are present.

The design of a table comes to mind. It should be designed with potential. It could be a social attractor, gathering people around it, a platform to stand on, a house for children to huddle under, a surface to dine on, to write on, to present things on, to make things on, to reflect on. It should have the potential to be and mean things that were not necessarily thought about in the design process. We think the steps to designing the table are to consider the place, and the materiality of the place, in which the table will exist. Then it could be tested by using various scenarios.

The Paju project is not a landscape design project; nor is it an urban design project. It is an infrastructural architectural project on a large scale – just as the table is on a small scale.

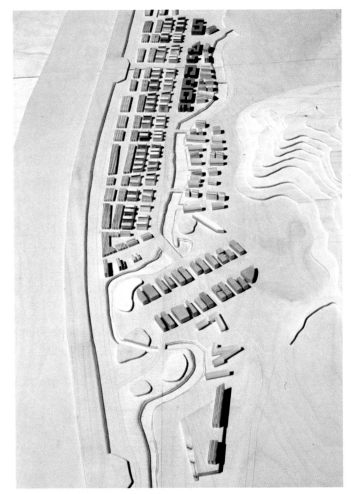

Design model of urban structures, Paju

Paju is a vague territory on the periphery of the city, a bit eerie and attractively enigmatic. It has something of the character of a wilderness, artificial and natural, and there is a feeling that it's necessary to tread carefully here and not do too much. We don't like to treat vague territories as *tabulae rasae*, as has happened too often in orthodox positivist approaches. Our method involves taking a step back and reading the history of these sites while suspending judgement.

The large space we have designed for Paju is a collage of the natural and artificial traces of different times: geological time, agricultural time, large-communication-infrastructure time, Cold War time, time-in-waiting, landfill time. We foster a state of coexistence with these traces. It is a site-specific territorial and temporal structure. It is a vessel of potential. We call it a landscape infrastructure. A landscape infrastructure is an urban topography that attracts development. It is a shared landscape foundation from which diversity and change can take off. You could say we are designing the rug and not necessarily the picnic, or the table but not necessarily the meal.

We like architectural infrastructures because they reveal the essence of architecture, they can be shared and they waken the imagination. We think they are a delightful aim for an architect in today's pluralistic practice.

Phenomenological Approach

Our approach might be called phenomenological. It is an approach to experiencing – subjective but shareable experiencing. It is not a functionalist approach that tends to forget the past and start from a *tabula rasa*. It is not the programmatic approach of orthodox modernity. It is an approach allowing discontinuity, an approach of coexistence, of operating next to each other at different times, of inhabitation of existing space. It generates improvisation, feelings, passion, wonder. Sensitive observation can become the proposition.

Credits
Paju City Design Manual
Architecture Research Unit (Florian Beigel, Philip Christou, Kim Tae Chul, Daniel Mallo Martinez and Park Chi Won, in collaboration with Kim Jong Kyu, Kim Young Joon, Min Hyun Sik, Seung Hchioh Sang).

Youl Hwa Dang Publishing House, Paju, Seoul, Korea
Architecture Research Unit (Bae Sang Soo, Florian Beigel, Philip Christou, Daniel Mallo Martinez and Park Chi Won, in collaboration with Kim Jong Kyu, MARU, Seoul).

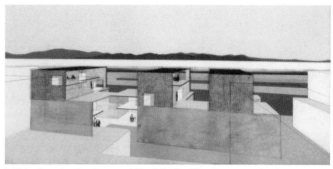

Initial collage showing the essential bookshelf building-form emanating from the concept of a street building with patios, supporting pavilions of the river horizon on top

Youl Hwa Dang Publishing House, construction photo, October 2003 (Kyounghwa Kang)

Since this essay was written, in November 2001, the construction of the Paju plan is very much under way. Phase I, consisting of 50 buildings, is almost complete. A number of international architects have been given the opportunity to contribute to the experiment of this place-specific and time-based approach to landscape urbanism. Youl Hwa Dang, the publishing house of Mr Yi, Chairman of Paju Book City, will be completed by Christmas 2003. This building is seen as a test case for the new methodology of the landscape infrastructure plan.

In Conversation with Michel Desvigne: Intermediate Landscapes

Perhaps we could begin by talking about your London project. The park you designed beside the Thames was intended to accommodate the Richard Rogers Partnership Millennium Dome in the short term and to form the heart of a new residential district in the future. What is the nature of this project, which seems to be attempting to reconstruct a primitive landscape out of a former industrial wasteland?

The Greenwich peninsula is in fact a meander of the Thames that was so badly polluted by previous industrial installations that it was necessary to strip the entire area to two metres below the existing ground level in order to decontaminate it. As a consequence, the project began with a radical site-clearance strategy. Given this starting point, the pursuit of a quasi-archaeological approach – seeking to reinstate historical marks on a *tabula rasa* site – seemed absurdly artificial. Equally, we rejected the idea of structuring the new park around the conventional stereotypical urban park forms that seemed to be suggested by the brief – the amphitheatre, pond, thematic gardens and monuments. Instead, by abandoning formal cues and cultural stereotypes, we were able to focus on reinventing the primeval substructure of the territory itself.

This approach required the invention of a powerful texture capable of giving quality to this formless environment – making the land habitable (by which I mean protected from the wind), framing the spectacular views and orientating the space. We wanted a texture against which forms and spaces could be created, but which would remain independent of the temporary layout of the 'millennium experience'.

Using references to geomorphological conditions of a similar scale and context, we imagined how nature itself might have colonized the site, and this conceptual starting point led to the proposal of a type of landscape texture modelled on the precedent of an alluvial forest. Our young forest, planted on a regular nursery grid, will develop in two successive phases, composed initially of a homogeneous stratum of 12,000 densely planted saplings, mainly hornbeams, out of which the spaces for the millennium experience have been sculpted. Over time this layer will thin out and be replaced by larger, nobler species – birch, alder, oak and willow – which will define the permanent spaces of the corridor. The more mature woods will themselves be sculpted according to future, unknown urban demands.

The exceptional temporal and physical scale of the project led to the creation of what I would call an intermediate landscape: a living landscape texture flexible enough to be integrated into a future urban context. This process appears to be comparable to the reconstruction of a natural landscape, but our starting point is explicitly artificial. We are playing with an architecture that relies on texture and variations of density rather than on composition of volume and mass, a process that endows this landscape with a 'naturalism' that is at odds with our cultural conventions, be they landscape or urban.

Could one consider the Greenwich project an attempt to implement an 'ecological treatment' of a territory?

I am currently heavily involved in teaching and research at Harvard. This work brings me into contact with professionals and students whose cultural approach to ecology is less technical and more ideological than our own. Ecology is considered above all else a method of deploying a living medium onto a given site in order to create a preconceived final form. This approach to nature is as different from our own as it is from the Germanic concept of a Romantic landscape. In fact, I am regularly surprised in the United States to encounter woods, prairies and marshlands in the heart of urban areas. These are artificial landscapes, and yet they are handled with a type of rusticity that is unknown in the language of European landscape architecture. The aesthetic of this American landscape, established by the likes of Frederick Law Olmsted, dates from the nineteenth century. It is far removed from the aesthetic of picturesque or naturalistic gardens: it seeks neither to re-create imagery from paintings nor to enforce ornamental principles, but proceeds from a desire to establish aesthetically pre-determined, authentic living environments. Unfortunately, contemporary American landscape architecture has strayed far from this culture, as marketing pressures tend to turn projects into overworked caricatures.

With my Harvard students we have taken on the derelict urban fringes of Boston, those abandoned areas next to roads, railways and industrial infrastructures, spaces that in fact belong to no official spatial categories. By mapping these sites, we have discovered that they make up a staggering 25 per cent of the overall urban area. In Europe we would typically seek to structure and integrate these voids by imposing order through grids and alignments. By contrast, the projects we have developed at Harvard tend to use modest and pragmatic means to evolve a new type of urban geography: making good the ground, decontaminating *in situ*, restoring the soil's fertility, diverting storm water and putting in place modest long-term maintenance strategies. These techniques encourage a progressive establishment of a powerful landscape on the abandoned sites. This type of natural process defines a parasitic landscape that is absorbed into the urban context at the geographical scale. The form of this landscape is more about process than composition.

Is the emphasis on technique in effect determining the aesthetic of the project?
The approach may seem technical, but it is rooted in the landscape traditions of the nineteenth century. The aesthetic is the aesthetic of transformation: the landscape develops as a product of processes of transformation, which are proposed and organized by the landscape architect. But it is true that these techniques do tend to result in a 'naturalistic' landscape – the woodlands, prairies and marshlands referred to earlier. In France we tend to impose order to improve the legibility (and functionality) of suburban areas. In this way, trees fill in for architecture, a grid of trees replacing a composition of facades.

The historic legitimacy of such practices (which across the Atlantic are described as *à la française*) is not actually proven. We tend to behave as if the classical models, and especially those of Haussmann, are our only means of dealing with suburban complexities. I find that these leaden references cloud the contemporary townscape and deny the opportunity of exploiting the real diversity and wealth of the environment. As to their capacity to improve the urban fabric, they seem rather feeble and irresolute.

One could define the American townscape as a vast suburb. However, the presence of this intriguing 'naturalistic' landscape holds some very pertinent lessons for improving the European suburbs: abundant planting that has developed a genuine geographical logic, with a grouping and spacing of trees that owes more to natural imperatives of soil, drainage and exposure than to artificial design. A 'naturalism' that when juxtaposed with a wholly functional and geometric form (such as a road) creates a true beauty of contrast. A landscape that develops a sense of unity, like a forest, within which built interventions are given their own genuine coherence. It is precisely this type of 'naturalistic' reference that we have proposed for the townscape of the Greenwich peninsula.

But is not this American 'naturalism' also related to the fact that it is a less worked landscape, a landscape less marked by human history?

This is not so true in the Northeast, between Boston and Washington, where densities approach those of Europe. There is a greater consciousness in the States of how urban contexts are actually fabricated. Children's books show how streets, pavements and urban services are built. The city is explicitly built on urban infrastructures. Buildings connect to these permanent infrastructures but are in a constant state of transformation. Paradoxically this pragmatism leaves nature a real part to play in the development of urban areas. This is not due to the continental scale of space found in the US or to its supposedly shorter history of human intervention, but has much more to do with a clearer distinction between what is created and what is given. In France, the town and country, our beautiful villages and historic centres, are all perceived as part of an overall heritage, but the management of development or conservation is divided among numerous organizations, so the overall 'collective' command of the process is inevitably weak. How else can one explain the type of passivity and inertia that has been the response to recent developments: the intrusive parcelling of sites, suburban sprawl, the proliferation of highways and the destruction of entrances to cities?

Is this absence of coordination of the built environment as relevant to the French suburbs as it is to the historic fabric?

The American suburbs are built in such a way that one never gets lost. By contrast, we are all constantly getting lost in French suburbs, because of the confusion of differing institutions:

a dedicated motorway, a national route, a departmental road, a municipal street, all functioning within their own logic and with their own architectural language – signage, fencing and pavements. When I travel, I move from the A2 to the N13 to the ring road to the D14 to finally arrive on an urban street. In the US, the system shows an overall consistency that stretches from the orthogonal division of the states themselves to the tightest urban street grid. In France, the process of fabrication has been rendered illegible by the institutions tasked with controlling the physical environment, and this confuses and overpowers all suburban projects.

What form should one give the landscape today?
Landscape has a preexisting form that in Europe appears to have been overwhelmed and rendered indecipherable. In the US, as in some developing countries, either through economy or pragmatism, the infrastructures and real-estate parcelling are so brutally superimposed onto the landscape that each of the different strata can be clearly discerned. This brutality, while sometimes horrific, can also be splendid, as it was in northern Italy. It results in a legible landscape. The situation in France is more complex, as the distinctions are blurred and confused, most notably in the large-scale motorway projects whose construction has more to do with politics than engineering. Abstract criteria are the guiding forces behind the imposition of these often grotesque physical interventions on the countryside.

The problem given to the landscape architect is to render the illogical logical, to integrate, to dissolve and to decorate with anecdotal interventions. Toll roads determine specific points of passage. These are then obliged to be connected to the existing town centres through 'gateways', which are notionally 'urbanized' with a palette of classical and Haussmannian devices. Faced with this very real confusion, it seems to me far more honest to clear, remove and clarify in order to regain the legibility of each stratum – nature, construction, infrastructure – in the process creating breathing space.

Does this type of 'aesthetic cleansing' seem to you the only possible modern approach?
I am totally convinced that it is the only way, and this has been the approach we have taken at three new stations on the TGV Mediterranean Line [Valence, Avignon, Marseilles]. The stations are all located on the fringes of cities in a landscape that is strongly fashioned by an

agricultural past but is now experiencing a phase of total transformation. Our work focused on recognizing, classifying, distilling and prioritizing the elements of the landscape. From this research we then create a new working language – the project ecology. For example, we exhumed from the mess of the Rhône Valley's urban peripheries the hedgerows, the orchards and the lines of plane trees, measuring and recording the proportions of these elements and translating them into our project. The enormous car parks of the TGV stations are treated as traditional orchards, grouped in a manner that is derived from the existing horticultural systems (albeit at a different scale). The car parks and buildings of the stations are thus grafted onto a system that stretches far beyond the actual site, into a total landscape that we would claim we are reactivating. Aesthetically, this is a game of substitution: the overall structure remains, but each individual element changes. This is not composition in the classical sense but a simultaneous insertion into and transformation of an existing landscape structure; there is no imposition of an exotic model but rather a transformation of indigenous elements.

In the Avignon project, this experiment has been extended beyond the confines of the station and into the whole area of the confluence of the Rhône and the Durance. A number of architectural teams are developing projects on the peninsula, and we, in our capacity as landscape architects, are acting as the custodians of the 'language'. Our brief is to support each team by recommending simplifications, clarifications and transformations that ensure that, at every level and scale, the legibility and the coherence of the landscape are conserved and reinforced.

Your TGV projects are possible because of the enormous political power of the client, but how can one proceed without political support and in landscapes whose coherence has already been seriously blurred?
I think one can find inspiration, again, from certain aspects of American landscape. The work of Olmsted seems particularly relevant and stimulating. Although we are all familiar with Central Park, in New York, I believe his less known and admittedly less spectacular work in Boston is of great contemporary relevance. Rather than simply designing the park as stated in his brief, Olmsted was drawn by the fact that Boston is built on an estuary whose maritime

rivers were silting up with sediment. He took this problem as the pretext for abandoning the notion of an ornamental park and instead implemented a real working landscape in the heart of the city, a landscape based on hydraulic requirements and made up of a system of dykes and basins capable of controlling storm water and sedimentation. Rather than proposing a conventional park on the surface and solving the technical problems underground, Olmsted used the rainwater itself to shape a true landscape, a topography that eventually determined the structure of the residential borough of Brookline in the suburbs of Boston. In a park treated as a functional landscape, the plants became, by necessity, part of the overall system of drainage and irrigation: where picturesque floral ornamentations were expected, Olmsted installed marshland and copses, and all this in the very heart of a city that was itself under construction.

Today's work with the Harvard students is to develop just such an approach, but this time in relation to the abandoned sites in Boston. We proposed transforming the problem of flooding into a virtue, an opportunity for the creation of a landscape: given that the railways and roads are located on floodplains, we designed ditches that follow the routes and terminate in basins dug into the industrial peripheries of town. There, as the maturing process develops, marshlands and poplar groves ensure good drainage and evaporation. Our objective is certainly not technical; but, perhaps ironically, technical and financial criteria have ended up legitimizing the construction of a coherent public landscape within a derelict area of suburban sprawl.

Is such an approach impossible in France?

France is a country where the role of the public sector is paramount – a situation that has no real parallel in the US. The French political system tends to generate large and grand projects – residential areas, business centres, elegant public parks – all geared towards integrating peripheral urban areas. Alas, it sometimes means waiting as much as 20 years before these proposals finally leave the drawing board, and in the meantime a whole generation has already grown up among the wasteland.

The approach we have taken in Boston and experimented with in London accepts the need to work with the temporary and the uncertain. In the absence of financial means or political will, we propose developing the vacant sites with rudimentary, agriculturally inspired techniques that establish a form of landscape with a geographical dimension. These sites are principally located around lines of infrastructure, together with which they form a coherent geography superimposed over the whole town.

The colonization by this temporary landscape gives these sites a powerful role to play in the transformation of the urban environment. At the very least it creates a temporary landscape that improves derelict areas. At the very best, and given that cities will develop around infrastructures, it could become a genuine catalyst for the regeneration of the suburbs.

Translated by Philip Gumuchdjian

PROTOTYPE ▶

A prototype is a contingent assemblage of relationships in a complex evolving system, and a stabilization in a process of iterative determination. It is constituted by relations between a varying number of components assembled in a collective dynamic with varying densities, loaded with reciprocal behaviours and instructed with motivations. Technical and functional constraints stiffen the armature of these relations towards a systemic regulation in protocols of responsive rules whose variations are nonessential and adaptive. Prototypes unfold as lineages from indexical organizations that evolve differentials in a process of organizational enrichment from raw conditions into robust ones. Indexing takes place via reverse engineering and adaptive differentiation, which develop through geometries capable of breaking down into interconnected geometric manifolds as they absorb information. Associated with systemic variables, sites can be understood and described as a multiplicity of circumstances that unfold as gradients in a dynamic field. Prototypes are their codifiers and markers, indicators of adequacy and registers of potentials, devices to steer order out of the circumstantial. Like an ongoing recipe-making, their brief is engineered through the continuous modification of a performance specification that tests and defines thresholds, absorbs feedbacks and regulates consistencies.–CN

Fragmentation and Clustering

Rather than working with predetermined housing typologies, a system of adaptation allows a range of configurations to emerge. The fragmentation of modules in a construction system accommodates topographic variations, infrastructural access and proximity to water, while also generating variants in the houses' internal organization. The ground holds the system together and restricts the free movement of modules, forcing the formation of clusters, small neighbourhoods and developmental units.

Yacira Blanco
Expansive Interfaces

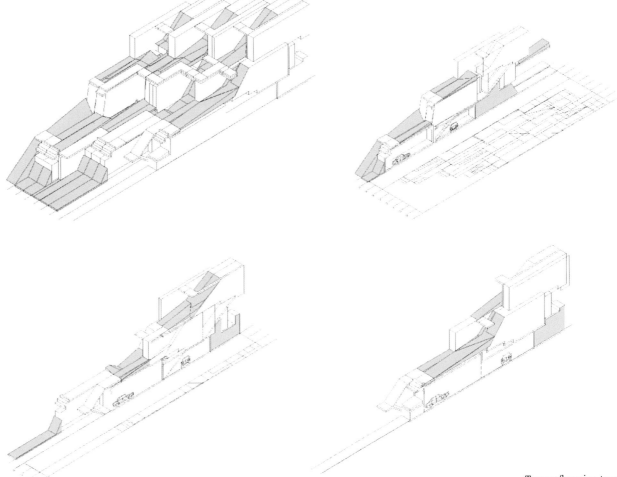

Terrace/housing types

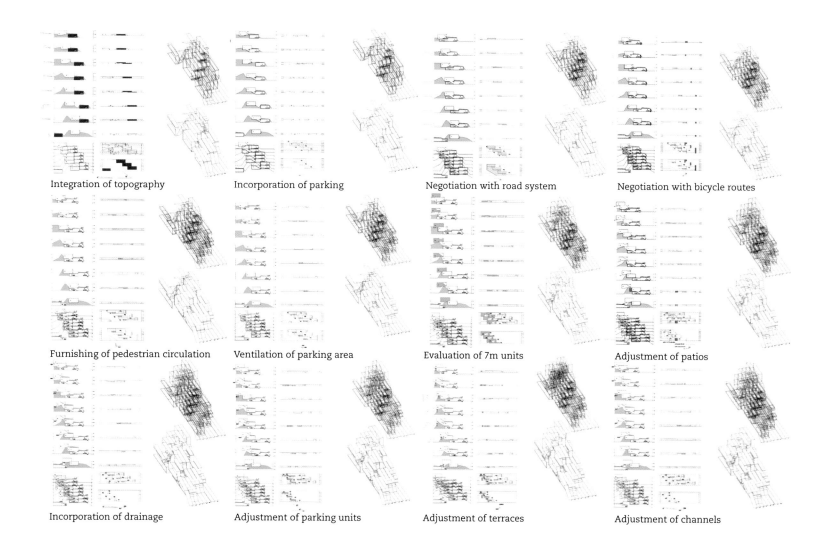

Integration of topography

Incorporation of parking

Negotiation with road system

Negotiation with bicycle routes

Furnishing of pedestrian circulation

Ventilation of parking area

Evaluation of 7m units

Adjustment of patios

Incorporation of drainage

Adjustment of parking units

Adjustment of terraces

Adjustment of channels

Selection and Modulation

Typological variants are produced and distributed in the space of the catalogue. The catalogue operates as a medium that incorporates and manages determinations, and as a ground that unfolds and adjusts varying evaluation criteria. The characteristics of the material organizations resulting from the differential catalogue are evaluated by defining and overlapping parameters, gradients and thresholds. Fit-enough assemblages are selected through readings on the zones of robustness or fragility of the system. These readings help to modulate the system's uptightness.

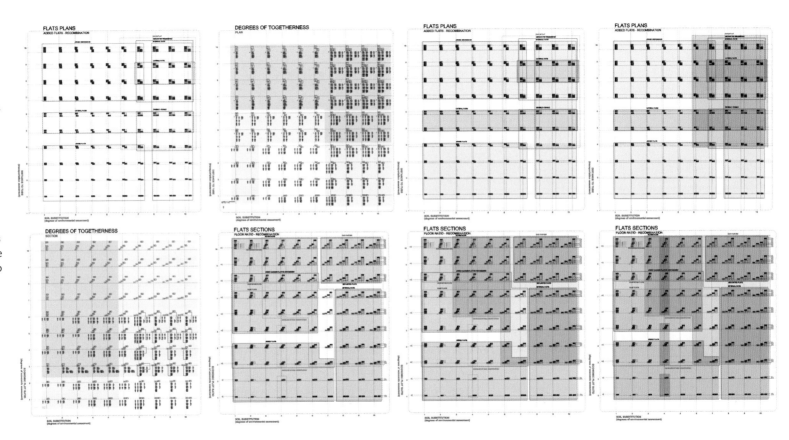

Armando Oliver-Suinaga
Situational Topography

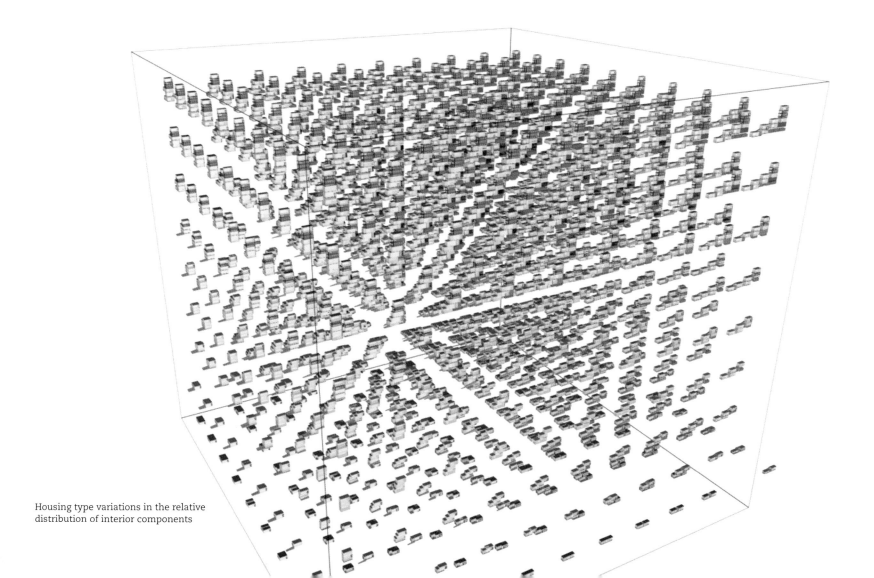

Housing type variations in the relative
distribution of interior components

Flexible Assemblage

Housing typologies are broken
down into dumb components
with flexible relationships and
simple modes of variation.
Responsive typologies with soft
thresholds emerge out of this
mechanism of assemblage.

Armando Oliver-Suinaga
Situational Topography

Regulation

An open deterministic mechanism regulates fluctuating demands for shopping and services and the unpredictable stages in the process of growth.

Enrichment

A shopping mall with public space restrictions is developed within one organizational system that intensely fragments components and deviates trajectories in a laminar organization. The organization sinks under the ground and the envelope gets absorbed in the laminar order. Different types of access from the surrounding areas integrate the organization into its context and force its enrichment in a process of progressive adaptation.

Simona Bencini
Windowscape

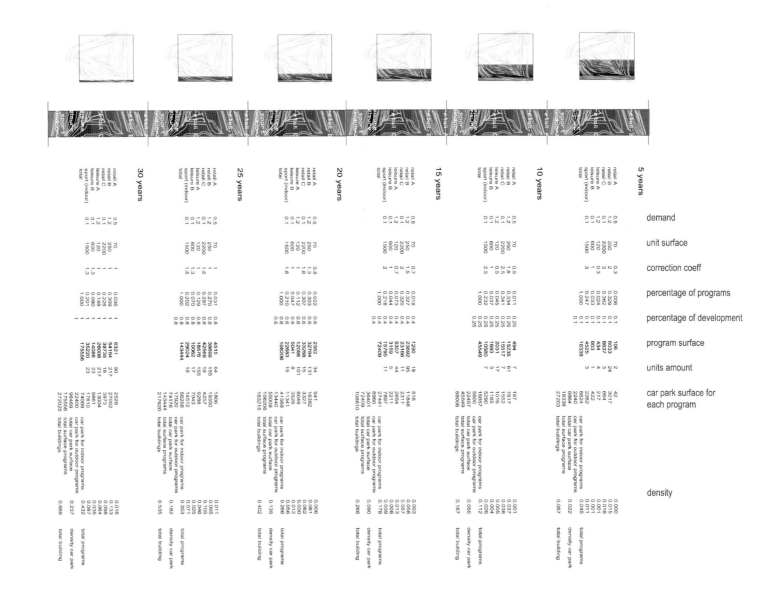

Field of potential markets

First displacement (river proximity)

Second displacement (access)

Field of commercial potentials

Vectors of displacement

Window displacement

Window placement

Escalator placement

Main circulation

Secondary connections

Fitting existing structures

Internal circulation pattern

Bundles of access

Sports facilities

Topographical differentiation

Vertical connections

Building structure and car park

Total circulation pattern

Absorption

The ground is constructed through a series of shallow parallel arches that index the vectors of a circulatory pattern. The vectorial arches curve horizontally, blend and acquire stiffness. The resulting differential mat is adjusted to absorb variations in density, edge treatments, circulatory and drainage patterns, and service distribution. Its structural rhythm is altered and proliferated.

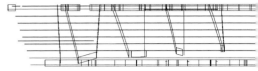

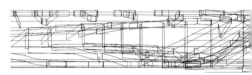

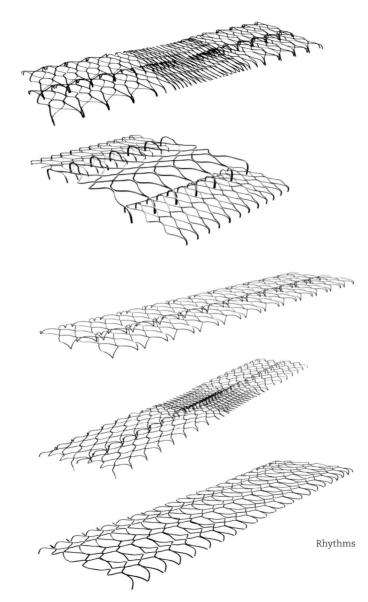

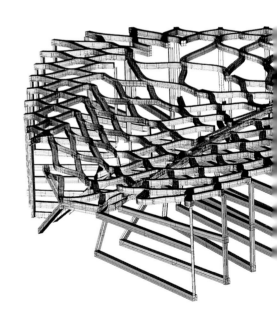

Rhythms

David Mah
Surface Matters

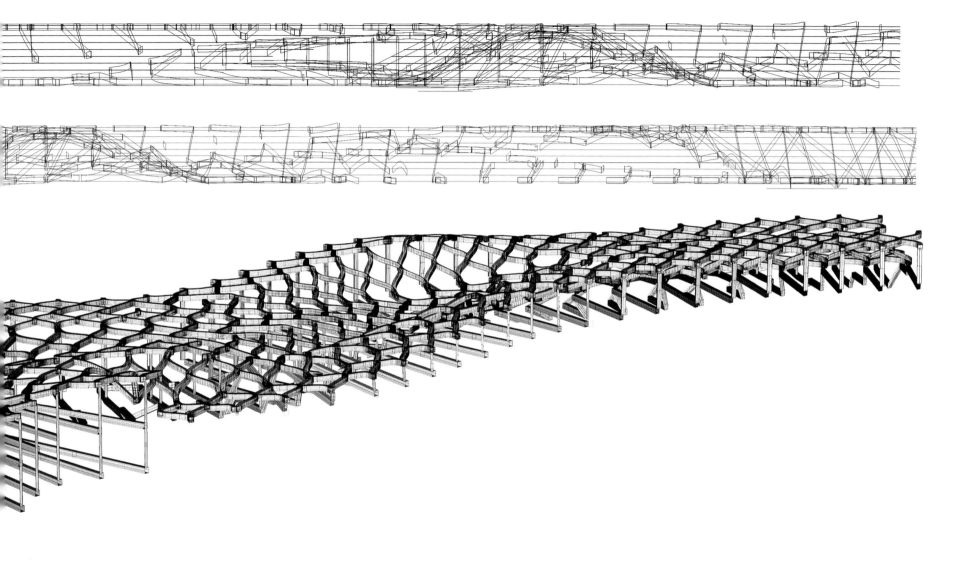

Proliferation

Circulatory strands are thickened, bifurcated in bundles, and segmented in repetitive rhythms in order to connect levels and accommodate services, furniture and structural components. The new multiplicity of subsystems is used to proliferate the system and increase its robustness through overspecificity.

Roxana Scorcelli
Urban Excess/River Access

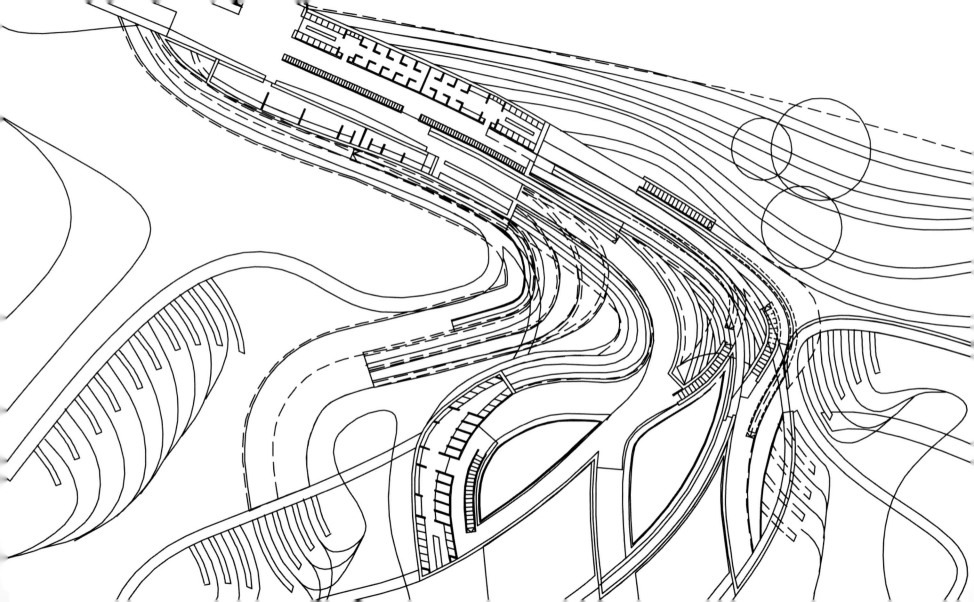

In Conversation with RUR: On Material Logics in Architecture, Landscape and Urbanism

Architectural theory, especially at Columbia, where you were teaching, has shifted away from questions of representation and issues of meaning towards the effects of architectural form. What do you think triggered this paradigm shift?

At one point there was a real hope that a truly transformative architecture would be possible through complex manipulations of representation. This came out of deconstruction and the whole legacy of semiotics in architecture. From the mid 1980s up to the early 1990s, these issues formed a central part of our project, but there was always a schizophrenic aspect to our design process. While we desired to make collage the engine of design, this was never entirely possible. For us, there was a kind of crisis that I could pin down to the work we showed in a publication called *Semiotexte Architecture*. We came to the conclusion that this kind of process was not really productive, that one was invariably going back to a more modernist way of composing or organizing, using bubble diagrams and then embellishing the project with secondary material that was image-based. Inevitably, the basic principles of organization would not and could not be linked to collage. This happened over and over again. We realized that we were just banging our heads against the wall. At that point we decided there had to be other ways of working. We were not the only ones frustrated by the process: across the board, people were becoming increasingly interested in projects that would engender change and difference within a coherent and integral system.

Has this had an influence on the role of perception of space in your design?

The semiotic approaches, of which collage is a part, primarily involved working with issues of perception and legibility. We realized that the perceptual condition was properly a by-product of the system, rather than the generator of it. The claim we would make is that one doesn't have to worry about perception, especially perception tied to the communication of a meaning: you will get all the perceptual effects, but you shouldn't start with these as the basis of a design – the question of perception within space follows from organization. Therefore, we are not denying meaning, but rather making it the project of the user rather than of the architect.

In your IFCCA West Side project you introduce a multitude of different activities and movements so that an uncontrollable site is created. Can this be seen as an attempt to simulate a complex natural environment where unforeseen conditions could emerge?

It really wasn't so much about replicating complex systems as engendering a certain complexity in the artefact. The assumption is that, by mixing systems, there is a greater possibility for unforeseen effects to occur in the final built structure. Our way of working involves managing different material regimes and systems. It incorporates multiple systems or environments into the mix and works back and forth between them. One of the overall ambitions of the project was for interconnectivity among all parts; there was an attempt literally to weave the strata of the city together. We tried to make these realms, which are already present on the site in some form, accessible and continuous, for example by incorporating green spaces, automobile infrastructure, different scales of structural hierarchy and pedestrian flow. We at first looked at fairly simple diagrams of movement from various infrastructural sources and then tested how these movements would mix in the station, in the commercial spaces and in the large event space, etc. Thus, we were managing an only partially controllable situation. Much of it had to do with working on something, seeing what would happen and then adjusting it along the way. Sanford Kwinter compared this way of working to husbandry, cooking or the way in which aerial combat is waged.

How can the notion of function and programme be expanded and become an essential input for the design process without submitting the design to a rationalist or opportunist procedure?

One of our basic assumptions is that there isn't a tight fit between programme and form. Functionalism is in itself a myth. We have known for quite some time that programme doesn't

IFCCA West Side

absolutely adhere to its supposed use. Labelling a space a kitchen and assuming that the only thing that happens in it is cooking is a fiction only certain architects believe in.

This is something that was already visible in the nineteenth century to people like Frederick Law Olmsted. Central Park is a great example of a loose fit of programme and form. Almost no programme is spelled out, and yet you could never say that it is aprogrammatic. It is actually loaded with different kinds of programmes, even though there were no labels as such on the drawings. Indeed, it continues to accrue different uses over time. Olmsted didn't know what rock concerts were because they hadn't been invented yet, but the spaces and the relations between roads and paths already provided for that scale of public event.

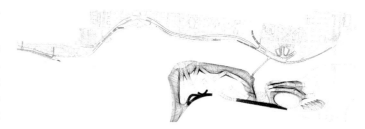

The modernist avant-garde had an ideal future in mind. Your IFCCA project seems to be more engaged with transforming the present conditions. Is there a desire to actively reconfigure the urban setting in the sense of a Utopian reinvention, or is the project seen as a mere catalyst for existing forces in the sense of a modification to the system?
I guess there still would be a Utopian impulse in the project, but it wouldn't be based on a model of a *tabula rasa* or a total reinvention of reality. That sort of conception of Utopia has exhausted itself anyway. A Utopian trajectory would be initiated, at least in part, from existing conditions out of which unforeseen outcomes might emerge. Our way of working differs from an acquiescent contextualism. In the [IFCCA] West Side project we were looking at the infrastructure on the site and then incorporating new organizations and environments. This process of incorporation could in a sense be linked to a Utopian desire, but it is very much based on operational techniques and material becomings.

Do you think of your projects as having a social impact? Is there a political agenda to your design that would allow it to become performative in a social manner?
The East River Corridor is probably our most obviously political project. We were looking at the area along the eastern shore of Manhattan and realized that a major roadway, the FDR Drive, blocks the city from its waterfront. We immediately noticed that in the wealthiest areas of Manhattan they had solved this problem quite elegantly, but had also isolated those places from the rest of the island. So what we proposed, based upon the existing Sutton Place

East River Corridor

solution, was to create continuity from the city to the edge. We also wanted to create a north-south continuity of public pedestrian space. This was the issue that really upset people, especially the inhabitants of the Upper East Side. In effect you would have people from Harlem and from Lower Manhattan passing freely into the areas of Sutton Place and other upscale neighbourhoods. These beautiful enclaves, the best parts of Manhattan, would be opened up to everyone on the island. In that sense the projects aren't simply abstract models: when implemented, they have a real political impact on the scale of the city. Also, at the programmatic level, it wouldn't be a matter of simply morphing one element into another. Our scheme very actively incorporates a lot of programme, which also upset people, because they would not simply get a continuous nineteenth-century park along the edge of the river. We suggested a lot of building mass and a lot of additional programme to make it a 24-hour space. The whole programme for revitalizing the edge of the city isn't simply about instituting a geometrical desire for continuous form. Equally, we don't see it as a critical approach, in the sense of merely revealing contradictions. It is an attempt to deal operatively and affirmatively with these conditions, and only then do they become political in a positive sense.

Looking at your IFCCA project, it seems as if the ideas of a performance-related space are influenced by an analysis of infrastructure. Do you use an instrumental logic to approximate your architecture to infrastructure?

There is an aspect of instrumentality in all of our work. In the design process, you need a certain level of determinacy in order to make a decision and to move ahead, but that doesn't mean that the end result would be absolutely deterministic. A building is organized by a whole series of hierarchical conditions of scale and use. We might have, for example, an infrastructural element at one scale and then try to mix it with other kinds of material and programmatic conditions. Naturally, these kinds of procedures require clear quantitative information that would then condition the development of formal and organizational strategies.

We were talking earlier about the flow of forces in the IFCCA project. How would these dynamic forces live on in the building?

Again, the question arises of how to deal with a dynamical system. We have increasingly

IFCCA West Side

moved away from a vectorial relationship between force, geometry and a derived materi-alization – which is what Greg Lynn would be interested in – to focus us towards working with the way matter computes itself. It is possible to create a dynamical field while operating on a physical model. Dynamics, although necessarily arrested in built structures, live in a very literal sense at the structural level.

This can be a way of shifting from dynamical organization into something that, even though static, is actively influencing organization and use beyond that of structure per se. This is not a metaphor; it is about a behaviour with which you could then manage architectural organization. For example, with the West Side project we were working back and forth between the programme within the roof and the roof structure itself by mixing the domains. The models were structural models, but we were already contaminating them with formal and organizational material. Thus force becomes a tool, an engine with which to influence and design in a structural field.

So it wouldn't be a purified structure, and it isn't really about innovative structural design either. You would not arrive at the most efficient structure possible given a certain span, but it would be as efficient as it could be given the inclusion of these other influences. So a modernist structural designer would probably consider what we were doing as impure and maybe irrational. We were trying to mix what, within a modernist framework, had been distinct realms.

We created a catenary field and then influenced it by impinging on it from many directions with lines of force. The idea for the catenary field came from a suggestion made by our structural engineer, Ysrael Seinuk. Antoni Gaudí used similar models in the design of the Sagrada Familia, though he was working solely with gravity forces, using loads on chain models that create simple parabolic arch forms automatically. Our situation was far more complex. We had generated a rough geometric model in the computer using the Alias modelling program (a program with the capacity to emulate forces on a geometry in a multidimensional field). The problem we were facing was that the computer model, while geometrically complex, was only a crude approximation of structural behaviour. Physical catenary models have the advantage of being able to compute geometry and structure simultaneously, with a high degree of precision. We proceeded to construct a two-metre-long chain model acted on by weights and pulleys. We were pulling on the chains from a number of directions in order to get them to correlate to the formal and organizational strategies of the building. This shaping resolved the organization of programmatic elements and the structural capacity of the field itself. The interesting part is that one could always be assured that any expression in this field was structurally sound. It is a material computation. A productive feedback existed between the material model and the work we were producing in the computer.

In your more recent projects, like the Kansai Library competition, your designs seem largely based on using the computer as a tool for the investigation and representation of three-dimensional structures.

We constantly work back and forth between physical models and computer models, only we generally haven't shown the process models in publications. We come from a slightly older generation that doesn't really trust computer-generated perspectival views. We are much more interested in the metrical space than in perspectival space, especially during the design process. We always want to have an artefact in front of us that can be inspected and measured.

For Kansai we initially used a bubble diagram as a model of connectivity among different programmatic zones. We then looked at the relationship of different slopes of floors and specific programmatic elements that would relate to those slopes. A provisional physical model was made from wax, which connects the topologies of these various surfaces of the ramp system. This was remodelled in the computer and analysed in terms of heights. After that we worked manually on a secondary scale by developing smaller organizations on the slopes as if we were working on a landscape project. So there is a constant alternation between media and methods, rather than a linear process.

Is it important to you that the process of form-generation and the forces that influenced it can be read and understood in the final project?

That is the kind of discussion we have had with Greg Lynn and Jeffrey Kipnis. It isn't so important for us to show the history of the project as a rational development. You know as

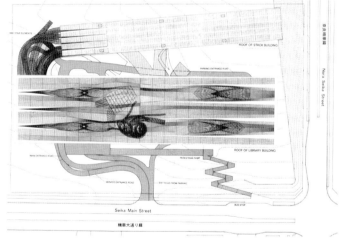

Kansai Library

well as I do that most of these are falsified histories anyway. The design is done and then a cosmetic history is presented that appears retrospectively as being rational. It is simply rhetoric to produce sanitized and rationalized histories, but it makes people feel better. That is not how our office works. The important thing to us would be to have those influences embodied in the project and not to simply make them a form of argumentation or description of a process. It doesn't have to be an illustration of those forces. I guess at the end it's about the project in terms of its actual effects and not the history of its process.

Some of the models for your IFCCA project contain three-dimensional flow diagrams. The architecture seems no longer to refer to a Cartesian model of a geometric, homogeneous and static space, but to be based on a notion of nomadic or transitory space.
Yes, that is substantially true. Essentially we are dealing with locales that are part of a vast global system, the transportation corridor. It is this movement corridor that concerns us, rather than the object itself moving. If we approach from the direction of the global logic – that is, from the vehicular side of things – then yes, the vectorial expression in the project as built form is actualized in use. However, from the standpoint of a pedestrian, that same formal development would appear to be more localized and more traditionally expressive.

But more generally, if we're talking about transition and the departure from static space, then time becomes a function of spatiality. Movement among temporal material regimes becomes a natural outcome of taking up the notion of the diagram as a productive procedure. Many different material dynamics begin to enter into the work, because now it is possible to move fluidly among them. So it is about a kind of extreme artifice – that is what I would call it. There is always the problem of representational thought, especially among critics. When critics say, you know, 'All of them are looking at weather', well, we are not really looking at weather. We are looking at weather in terms of its dynamics. But it always has to be expressed in the terms that are possible in the material construct of architecture. And in that sense, one could further claim that such diagrams do not really originate in weather either, that there is a vectorial dynamic that crosses many different material systems. This, of course, did come up in the sciences: one of the realizations in thermodynamics was that there was a way of generalizing apparently disparate kinds of material and physical behaviours through a common dynamic. So we could make a similar claim, especially since we consider architecture to be another material system, even if it is an artificial one, consciously created rather than found in nature.

The Water Garden project is a special case of diagrammatic behaviour, for the effects of water were manipulated directly (what Jeffrey Kipnis terms diagrammatic 'realism') and also carried over into the organization of other materials, like concrete and grass. It was in effect an attempt to harness a range of different kinds of geometries in relation to the behaviour of the water. First we established a cross-sectional geometry that is really distinct from the way the grooves of the garden are projected. These grooves, an ogival geometry in a cross section, belong more to the Cartesian side of the geometry, except that it already has built into itself a kind of acceleration. From the base to the point of the ogive there is an effect of acceleration as the water rises or lowers. So there is a mixing of the use of a Cartesian type of geometry and a topological geometry, which was expressed in the projection of the ogival cross-section as they comprise the form of the grooves. Above all, our interest was to produce certain effects of flow in the medium of the water as well as in the garden itself, so that there would be an indexical relationship between the static form and the flows within it.

How can a building be active and have a potential for activity, and how can time become operative within the IFCCA project as built architecture?
Infrastructure is inherently connected to flow and quantity (10,000 people an hour flowing into and out of the station, etc.). In the crudest possible analogy, if you are handed a high-pressure hose with water flowing out of it, it's not a question of imagining its activity and force but of what to do with it and how to direct it. Therefore architecture, although physically static, enters into these conditions through organization. Equally, there are effects that, while tied to quantitative conditions, are in themselves not reducible to pure data. The time that becomes operative in a building, for example, is not clock time, measurable like time on a stopwatch, but rather duration, which is about how environments affect experience. However, we would contend that quantitative material organization is generative of these experiences, but not the other way around.

Finally, it must be emphasized that time, especially in relation to activity or potential activity in a project, is unthinkable and becomes an empty abstraction when separated from an actual site or proposal. We do not subscribe to the concept that time or any other value or series of values can be manipulated or staged without an intersection with material conditions. A rather extensive body of work by a number of contemporary practitioners has dealt with datascapes as a way of approaching the design of cities. I believe this direction in architecture was first put forward by Rem Koolhaas, in his well-known diagram coordinating time and use in his proposal for the city of Yokohama. What is important there is the fact that this early datascape was generated in parallel with the proposal or indeed after the design was under way. It was not in itself generative. Adherents and followers of this method have attempted to utilize these sophisticated graphing techniques as the sole basis for urban design projects. Inevitably a crisis ensues in such work when it comes to formalizing the proposal. In the worst of cases the data is reified – essentially building the graph. At best it becomes an impoverished preliminary to designs that in reality can never be reduced to the datasets themselves. But to get back to the issue of the temporal: time, like any other quantity, is inherent in any material field, be it a field of battle or a field of flowers. Indeed, the city is just such a field. Urban proposals, in order to be effective, must arise from the ebbs and flows of a field that incorporates the exchanges between data, proposition and place.

Michael Hensel

Ocean North – Surface Ecologies

What is landscape urbanism? The argument pursued herein starts from the position that this emergent discipline is not primarily about a sort of landscape gestalt – making cities look like landscape – but rather entails a shift in emphasis from the figure-ground composition of urban fabric towards conceiving urban surface as a generative field that facilitates and organizes dynamic relations between the conditions it hosts. This addresses in particular the interactions between the built environment – with articulated surfaces as its medium – and the subject, both individually and collectively. With this notion of surface potential and surface activation, two interesting questions arise: by what means can the project of dynamic surface activation escape the legacy of traditional object-design – the designer's finite engagement with the product – and engage instead with the open-ended, heterogeneous and temporal relation between subject and surface as a way of space-making? In what way can such an alternative approach to design acknowledge and incorporate indeterminability and contingencies relative to the way in which material surfaces might be appropriated, without merely becoming incoherent problem-solving actions?

Starting from these questions, Ocean North has developed an approach to design that engages more directly with the dynamics of the built environment. The practice pursues an 'ecological' design paradigm – not 'green', but organizational – that emphasizes temporal relations and interaction between subject and milieu. Our approach stresses the interrelational makeup of the environment as a continually unfolding generative field. An instrumental enquiry into the interrelation of the provision made by the built environment and its performative potential necessitates a geometric taxonomy of surfaces. This taxonomy in turn yields a notion of 'surface ecology', which links specific material form to its real-time use by the subject.

Ocean North's particular approach to surface potentials commences with the disjunction of the geometric articulation of material form from the deliberate encoding of implied representation or meaning in order to instil what Roberto Mangabeira Unger and Jeff Kipnis refer to as 'blankness'.[1] This notion implies formal abstraction that aims at engaging in unexpected formal and semiotic affiliations and relations between subject and surface without settling into fixed alignments. In pursuing this notion, we deploy computational methods of sampling and fusing partial geometries into unfamiliar and nondecomposable geometric composites.[2] This operation enables typological references to be removed from the resultant form and the space defined by it. As meaning is replaced as the predominant operative encoding of geometry, emergent orders arise from the real-time interaction between the space defined by the new composite form and the beholder. In this way geometric ambiguity shifts the emphasis from structure as static material-arrangement to the dynamic structuring of mobile relations in time and across space.

One example of this approach is the Extraterrain furniture project (1996), which aimed at charging a simple material surface with varied potential for use while at the same time evading any prescription or indication of an intended proper use. Various sectional geometries were digitally sampled and fused into a nondecomposable surface in order to arrive at a composite geometry free of referential associations to any furniture types. Computational modelling allowed for a rapid reassemblage of the sampled geometries in order to assess the resultant composite geometry's latent ergonomic capacity. The final piece was made out of a vacuum-formed sheet of ABS plastic, which was subsequently reinforced with a sprayed-on layer of polyurethane.

Unlike the soft-surface environments of the 1960s and 1970s, Extraterrain offers an experiential landscape made of an unusually hard surface. This implies that the soft human body has to adapt to the surface articulation of the object, repositioning itself frequently in search of comfortable positions. From the need for repositioning arises the necessity of negotiating the surface area with other occupants. The relatively large size of the piece, which makes co-occupation possible, is an important characteristic. This condition, together with a lack of demarcation lines indicating individually assigned zones, yields a need for ongoing 'territorial' negotiations. Furthermore, the undulating and folding of the surface rules out the

Extraterrain

112

1 Roberto Mangabeira Ungers, 'Towards the Better Futures of Architecture', in *Anyone* (Rizzoli: 1991); Jeff Kipnis, 'Towards a New Architecture, Folding in Architecture', in *AD*, 1993.
2 This digital animation technique was first deployed for the Ocean North entry to the Time Capsules competition organized by *The New York Times* in 1998. For reference, see Michael Hensel and Kivi Sotamaa, 'Vigorous Environments', in Ali Rahim (ed.), *Contemporary Techniques in Architecture* (Wiley: 2002).

creation of privileged positions. Subtle or abrupt shifts produce a continued reconfiguration of the space of Extraterrain, as experienced by its occupant(s). The way, then, that the surface might be occupied depends on the individual user's characteristics – age, weight, size, fitness, imagination – and on their willingness to discover 'body techniques' to occupy the piece. Body technique refers to the exploration of an object's surface geometry for common sitting positions as well as new body positions that might suit the object's shape and available space. In this way, geometry and positioning trigger incidental individual use, with the array of individual use accumulating to collective interaction. The latter constitutes an unfolding field for social interaction yielded by the geometric articulation of the surface.

The competition entry for the Töölö Open Arena (Helsinki, 1997) transposes this research into surface articulation and occupation potential onto a much larger architectural scale. The site for the arena lies north of Helsinki's centre, on the axis of Kiasma – Stephen Holl's Museum of Contemporary Art – and Alvar Aalto's Finlandia Hall, with natural park landscape and the Olympic Stadium to the east and residential urban fabric to the west. Generated from site-specific activities, the scheme consists of three topographically articulated surfaces that link Helsinki's urban fabric to the natural park landscape. These surfaces allow for free circulation and programmatic distribution between each other and the site, thus making it possible to extend informal park activities onto the surfaces of the arena at times when no ticketed sports events are taking place. This approach opens up the vast space of the stadium to various formal and informal programmatic strata of the city. A productive tension between programmed and nonprogrammed surfaces arises from the programme distribution and the articulated topography of the seating, organized as clusters of seats that become naturally situated on the articulated surfaces. In this way the scheme facilitates an experiential tension between individual and collective habitation, much as in the Extraterrain project.

The Intencities installation (Helsinki, 2000) pursued this approach further and deployed a broader palette of elements, influences and relational dynamics in order to achieve a richer scope of interactions. The project was designed as part of the Helsinki Cultural Capital 2000 events. The site for the intervention was Makasiini, a nineteenth-century, single-storey U-shaped block of ex-railway depots facing the Finnish House of Parliament and Kiasma. The intervention incorporated elements of art, architecture, dance, music, media and graphic

Töölö Open Arena, Helsinki

design. The multidisciplinary design team devised a loosely coupled choreographic layout that engendered dynamic interactions between scheduled performances – formal, sonic, tactile – and material elements, as well as emergent flows of movement, events and ambient effects across the site. The architectural component of the intervention comprised six geometrically differentiated structures made of steel tubing, timber planks and plastic film.

The structures made loose provision for programmatic arrangements, such as stages, seating or circulation areas, viewing platforms and bridges, while at the same time avoiding functional representation. These structures revealed their usefulness only through the staging of events and artistic performances, exposed to spontaneous use by the artists, visitors and audiences. The construction and surfacing of the structures was undertaken over time, with their appearance and presence changing onsite. Motion-triggered light and sound systems were integrated into the structures and enabled a feedback relation between visitors and the changing ambient effects of the intervention. In providing a projection surface, the structures configured an audiovisually animated landscape as well as both stage and backdrop for the different events and performances. The introduction of new media technology served to translate physical movement across the site into digital animations, which were projected onto the surfaces of the structures. Visitors could make use of both their actual movement and their mobile phones to manipulate the projected graphics, thereby altering the audiovisual appearance of the intervention. The dance performances evolved randomly in relation to visitor movement and surface articulation. The initial spatial distance and distinction between dancers and audience gradually decreased as the dancers moved into, through and with the audience, making use of the narrow space of a bridge structure. Through this open choreography the audience became an active and integral part of the performance. Overall, this individual and collective movement of visitors and performers, combined with the differentiated geometry of the material construct and the changing intensities of ambient effects, acted to assemble and disperse the elements of the intervention into constantly changing configurations. The built and ambient environment, events and deployed technology jointly produced a field of conditions and effects animated by collective inhabitation.

The deployment of contingency in the Extraterrain, Töölö Open Arena and Intencities projects is obviously in opposition to traditional design approaches, which require the

Intencities, Helsinki

114

asserton of hard control over relationships between matter and functionality. Engaging relational dynamics therefore entails material interventions in continual processes, and the registration and examination of emergent temporal relations between subject and environment as well as their combined feedback effect upon the intervention. Feedback, then, informs the careful modification of the regulatory influence and changes the kind and degree of control over the transformation of the milieu, establishing the organizational dynamic and heterogeneity that characterizes the ecological-design paradigm.

So, to summarize the argument: interventions along this paradigm proceed by setting out fields of possible arrangements between subject and surface. Constituting generative fields – surface ecologies – they emanate from the varied tensions between nonprescriptive, yet directed, relations between milieu, intervention and subject, in a perpetual process of destabilization and restabilization. The actual elements of emergent affiliations between intervention, milieu and subject are the milieu's manifold formal, material and ambient elements, which produce effects perceived by the subject. In turn, the actual effects and the reactions of the subject have a combined impact upon the milieu. Performativity arises from dynamic feedback relations between the subject and the milieu, emanating from site-specificity and the real-time engagement of the subject. It is crucial, however, to distinguish here between the concept of the *Gesamtkunstwerk* as a totality and the pursued notion of designing with relational dynamics. The difference is simply given by (a) the implicit and accepted incompleteness of the latter; (b) its ability to incorporate contingency and the accidental into a continual generative process; and (c) to graft itself onto a mobile – thus incomplete – context. The following two projects – one horizontal, the other vertical – continue the speculation on relational dynamics on a much larger scale.

Commissioned by the NRW (the Forum for Culture and Economy), the study for the Landsc[r]aper Urban Ring Bridge across the River Rhine (Düsseldorf, 2000) was based on the supposition that an inhabitable bridge of the required scale is only viable when it engages intensively with the programmatic and demographic strata of the urban matrix. Hence urban connectivity, intensification and projected performance are of central concern to the scheme. The proposal aims at a tactical development of organizational structures that provide transitions between diverse locations and programmes across a multitude of scales. In doing

Landsc[r]aper Urban Ring Bridge, Düsseldorf

so, it condenses and bundles programmatic and infrastructural trajectories so as to induce various types of movement, thereby mixing different populations and sustaining differential inner-urban life and social interaction.

The scheme consists of three coupled organizational systems. An outer urban ring links existing infrastructural routes in a system that organizes the traffic both around and into the city centre while relieving the latter from through-traffic. An intermediate-scale urban ring links and completes existing programmatic and infrastructural conditions around a relieved city centre, linking the Altstadt with Oberkassel across the river. This ring directs pedestrian flow, stimulated by the deployment of public transport. Tramlines and a trolley-bus system increase the circulation along the perimeter of the city centre. An inner urban ring combines and bundles urban programmes on a pedestrian scale, drawing maximum benefit from its proximity to the river. A continuous pedestrian promenade provides for a rich palette of public spaces and programmes along and across the river, and seasonally incorporates the programmable Oberkasseler floodplain, with the modified floodplain offering diversely programmable surfaces. A continuous landscape ring combines green spaces with indoor and outdoor sports and leisure facilities. This northern segment of the ring is the Landsc[r]aper Bridge, which couples leisure and cultural programmes with public and vehicular infrastructure into programmatic links between the two sides of the river, while at the same time becoming an urban destination. The various programmes are organized in bands along the length of the bridge in order to enable choices between undisrupted engagement with a particular programme or possible transitions between programmes along a trajectory of pedestrian movement. It is a central element of the scheme that provisionally programmed surfaces are interlinked with nonprogrammed ones. Both conditions allow for urban activities to emerge between the new and the existing, and in response to demographic trends and tendencies. The new bridge deploys a geometrically varied arch-and-beam structure and moveable building skins that provide enclosure. Its differentiated geometry serves as a cognitive element that enhances orientation when moving through it. Comprising an assemblage of multiple, related structural systems and material envelopes, this very large and complex structure introduces a landmark to Düsseldorf that reflects the heterogeneous, dynamic and progressive culture of the city and its inner-urban infrastructural landscape.

World Center for Human Concerns, New York, this page and opposite

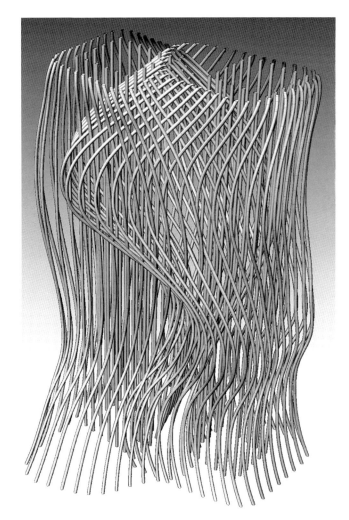

The study for a new World Trade Center for New York, commissioned by the Max Protech Gallery, proposes a World Center for Human Concerns (2001), a space for all peoples and cultures. The volume of the proposed building provokes a strangely suggestive and sensuous, if abstract, image of formation, continuity and multiplicity. It remains intelligible whether a single object folds upon itself or divides, or whether two objects are entwined in conflict or fusion. As a memorial to September 11, 2001, and a statement against all acts of violence, the volume of the new World Center inscribes within itself the volume of the previous Twin Towers, which are visible as vague figures through the new building's textured and folded skins. The spaces of the World Center result from the draping and folding of the building skin, which articulate a set of interstitial spaces that do not follow or prescribe any particular spatial hierarchy. Instead, the resultant spatial residues and pockets await their programmatic articulation, either in subsequent design phases, in collaboration with other designers, experts and participants, or, to a greater extent, in real-time, through a shifting pattern of collective inhabitation and appropriation. Through its ambiguous geometric articulation and lack of prescribed programme, the scheme seeks at this stage to be provocative and projective towards emergent and temporal social and institutional arrangements. In order to achieve this condition, it pursues a strategy of spatial differentiation via the material articulation of the building skin rather than by vertical programmatic zoning. Its surface geometry articulates the spatial pockets that result from the draping and layering of the building skin, while its material makeup and striated articulation – similar to that of the previous Twin Towers – allow for a modulated transparency of both the skin and the spaces within and beyond it. The tension between blankness and articulation, continuity and multiplicity, of the object yields differentiated dynamic relations between the object and the beholder. Every viewpoint and location becomes from the onset special and nondiscriminated.

The scheme relinquishes the common high-rise organization based on central service and circulation cores, but utilizes instead the building skin as a space for circulation, with a large number of circulation channels nested within it. The surplus of circulation space and channels throughout the entire building skin provokes a redefinition of programmable circulation as a social and experiential space, as well as easing evacuation.

This scheme makes possible an alternative approach to urban densification in Manhattan.

The method of draping building skins can be extended to existing structures in the form of 'parasite' buildings. In place of the obvious difficulties with vertical growth (and the impossibility of horizontal expansion), the study proposes thickening the space of existing buildings by adding layers around them. With this approach, it is necessary to revise strategies for getting daylight into deep plans and structures. The scheme approaches this problem by questioning an undifferentiated need for daylight, looking at how differentiated interior habitats could be articulated in relation to the amount of available daylight. The rainforest and the oceans, where microecologies flourish even at the lowest regions, might serve as an analogical model. This analogy can inform a reformulation of what might constitute a 24-hour city. So far this notion implies retail, leisure and entertainment programmes available around the clock. An alternative definition might imply 24-hour-daylight conditions. The darker core of deep volumes might constitute a 24-hour night-programme zone, while the outer and peripheral areas might enable a flexible negotiation of programmes relative to changing or artificially suspended daylight conditions. A related time-structure relative to global time zones could respond to the different needs of the peoples and cultures that may occupy the World Center and similarly deep structures.

How could one then imagine a further surface articulation, potential and activation of such large structures? In some ways, the Extraterrain and Intencities projects might suggest a possible scheme for a finer and perhaps temporal surface articulation that can affect various scales and make provision without prescription. In this way Ocean North's work suggests a strong move away from the common belief that only the undifferentiated open-plan organization offers the utmost freedom for flexible programming of spaces. The scale-spanning and time-based approach that emerges with articulated and activated surfaces – surface ecology – could then be one possible marker of landscape urbanism.

The machinic plan constitutes a transversal intelligence, or metapractice, that disregards the strategic as a top-down mechanism of control and prediction, and reframes it in a process of systematic idealization and breeding over time. Rather than perpetuating the model that understands the generic as transcendent and detached from the contingent, the accidental and the local, the machinic plan develops generality through the management of abundance, organizational variation and performative resilience. It is not preconceived as an ideal but generated as a potential. Thus concerned with overspecificity rather than with neutrality, it regards difference as the ultimate source of robustness and as the grain for its internal normativity. The machinic plan sieves the fluctuation of the rationale under which the urban project operates through the management of forces, resources, concerns and negotiations, building up a broader effectiveness than that of the masterplan. Its systematicity results from the development of a virtual code constituted by protocols that allow communication across domains and transmission between scales, so that causes and effects cascade, assuring its sustenance and survival.–CN

Mesh-Frame

A mesh of circulatory bifurcations and a triangulated structure frame the differential distribution and changes in the mix of farming, leisure and market units.

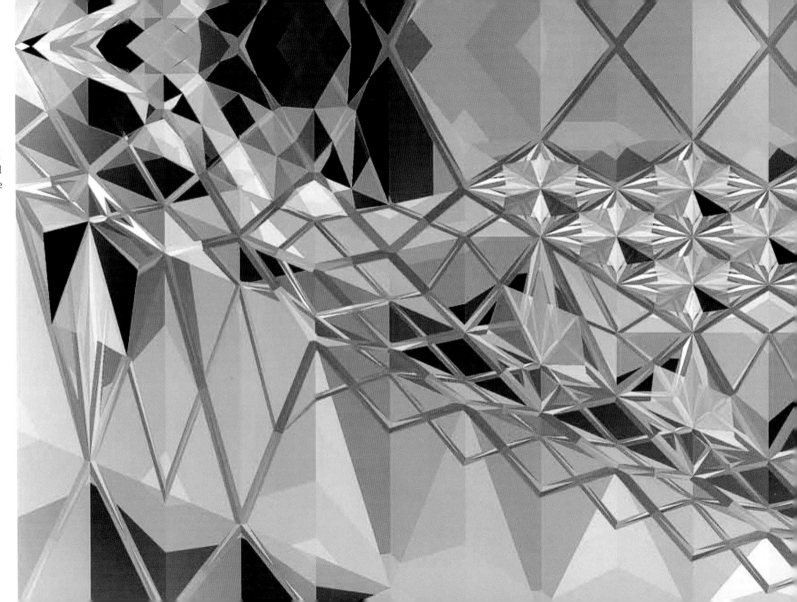

Santiago Bozzola
Changing Structures

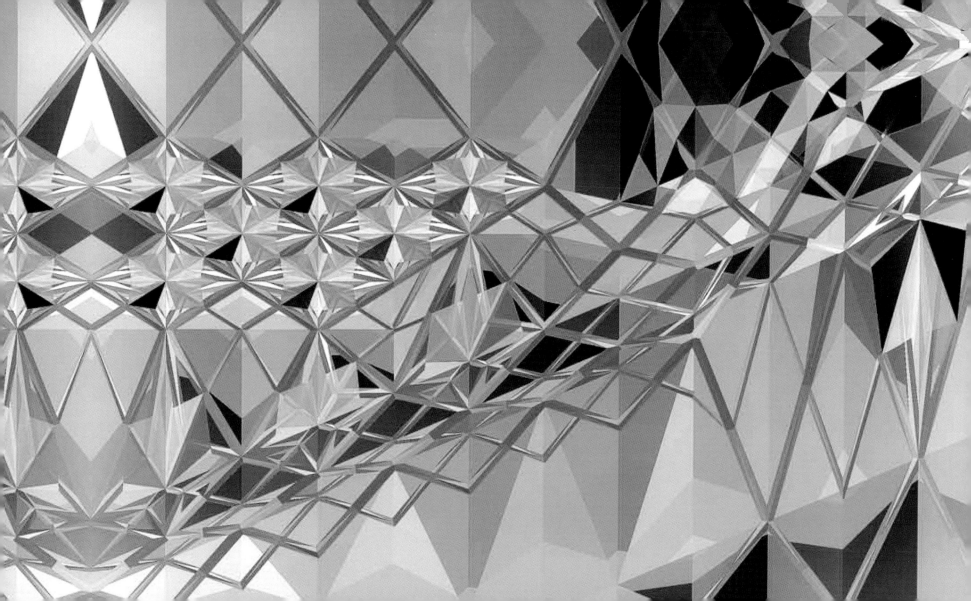

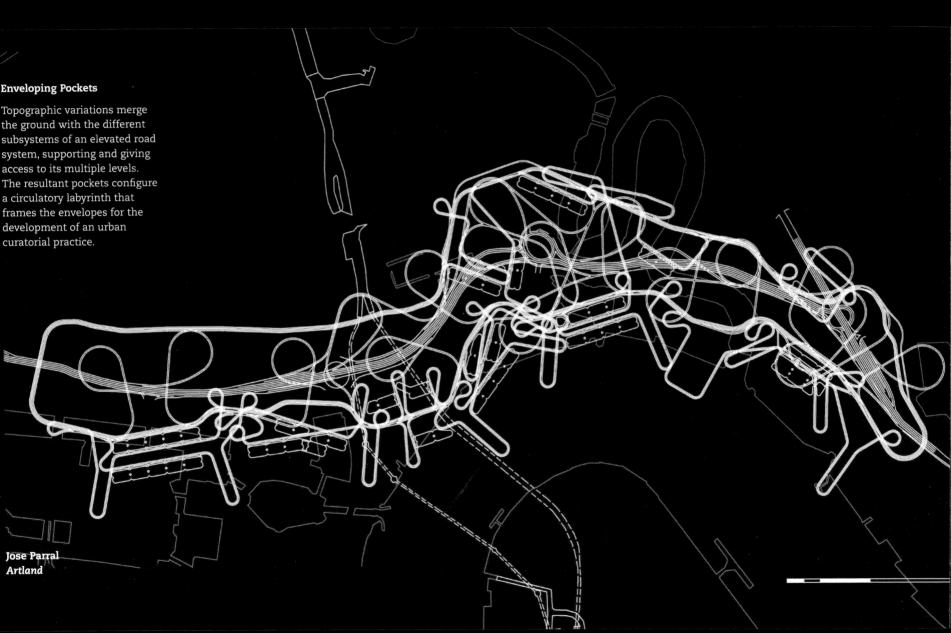

Enveloping Pockets

Topographic variations merge
the ground with the different
subsystems of an elevated road
system, supporting and giving
access to its multiple levels.
The resultant pockets configure
a circulatory labyrinth that
frames the envelopes for the
development of an urban
curatorial practice.

Jose Parral
Artland

0   500m

Pattern Intensification

A decentralized circulatory system follows the variations and accidents of a continuous pattern of terraced housing. Each of its subsystems intensifies its identity by exaggerating constraints and tendencies. Parallel series, clusters, neighbourhoods and regions are qualified in this process. The system stays open and integrated, while its responsiveness to various developmental scenarios increases.

Yacira Blanco
Expansive Interfaces

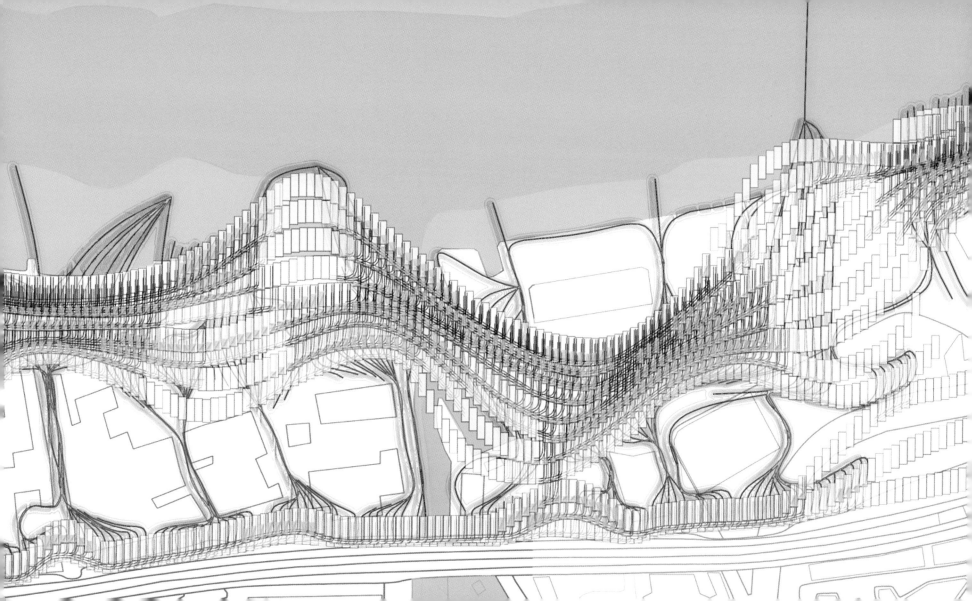

Textural Modulations

The ground's surface is divided into two interconnected systems: one textural, modulating its faces, and the other structural, integrating its inner rhythm. An intensively mounded surface varies in thickness in order to manage water drainage on the upper side and space height on the lower. A structural net blends structural components and integrates them with the organization of shopping and leisure corridors.

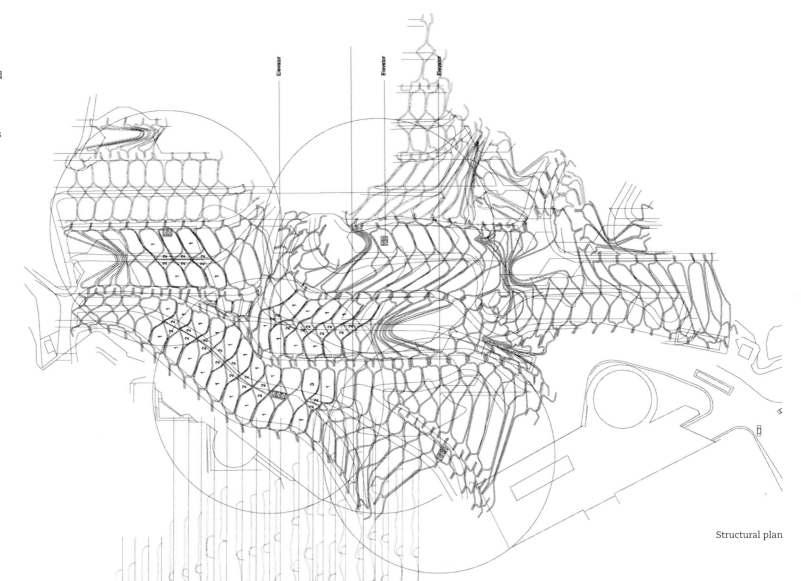

David Mah
Surface Matters

Structural plan

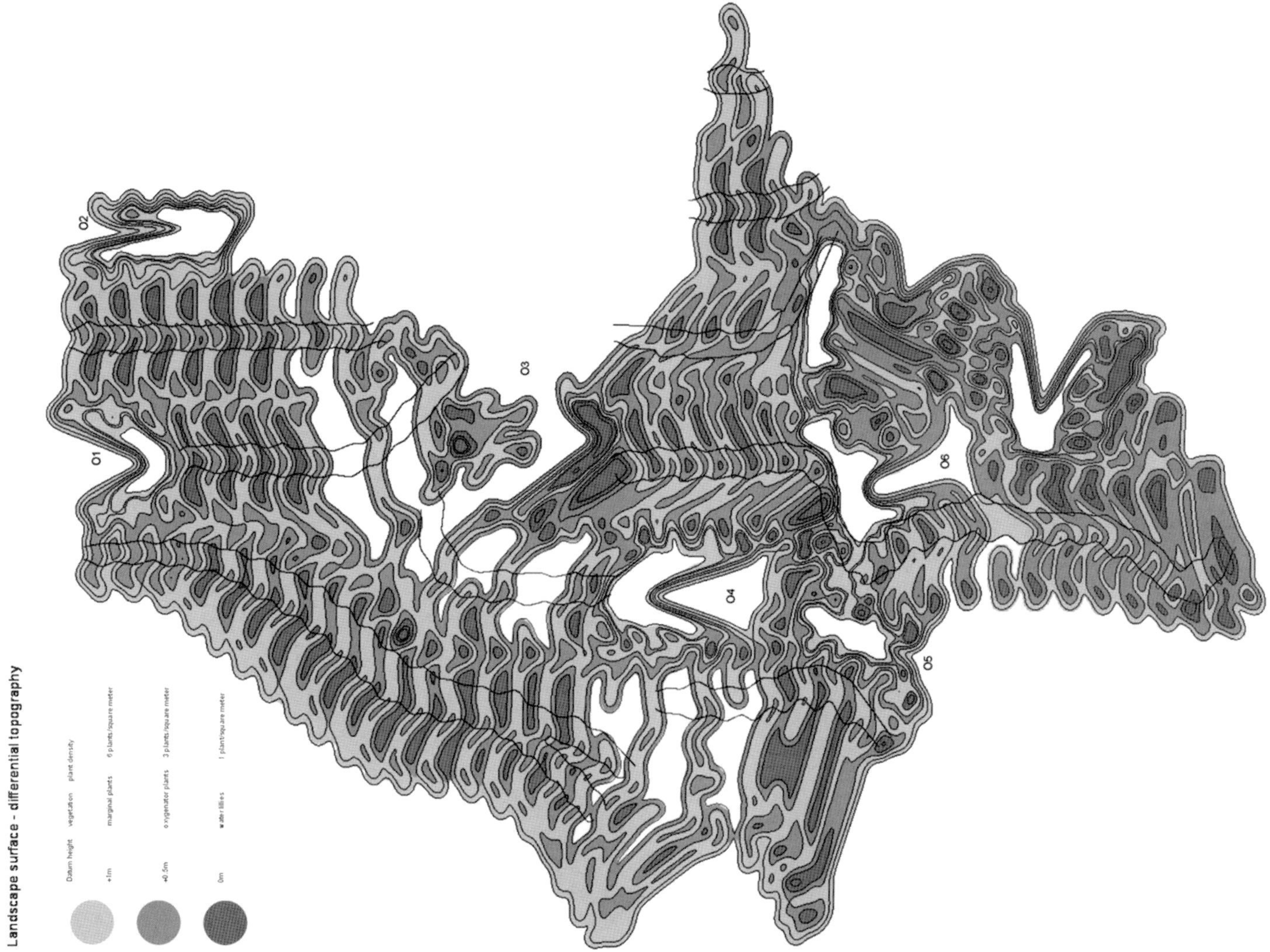

Landscape surface - differential topography

Datum height   vegetation   plant density

+1m   marginal plants   6 plants/square meter

+0.5m   oxygenator plants   3 plants/square meter

0m   water lillies   1 plant/square meter

O1

O2

O3

O4

O5

O6

Textural plan

Linear Erasure

Corridors running between
infrastructural nodes restrict
and activate the spread of
housing components in a
process of selective linear
erasure.

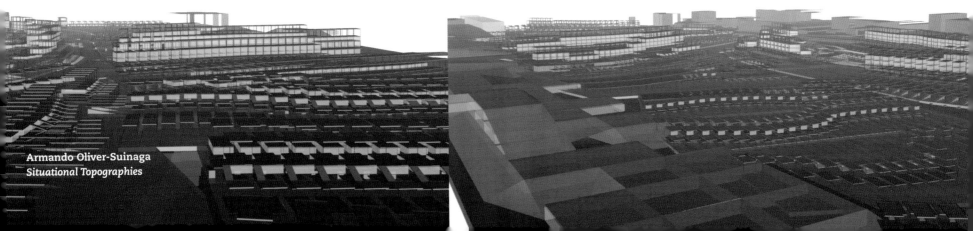

Armando Oliver-Suinaga
Situational Topographies

Additive Folds

Striated by multiple
circulations, segregated in
three layered surfaces,
subdivided and diversified in
triangular patches, integrated
in a single developmental
mesh and networked as a
space-frame continuum, the
ground is finally reconfigured
as an additive mille-feuille
system of folded faces.

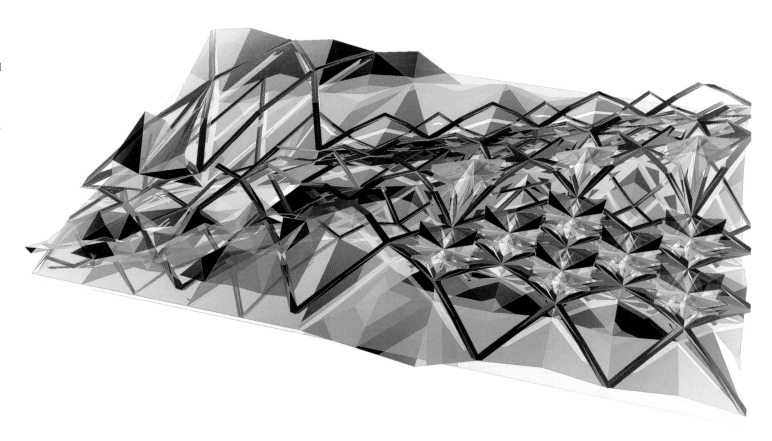

Santiago Bozzola
Changing Structures

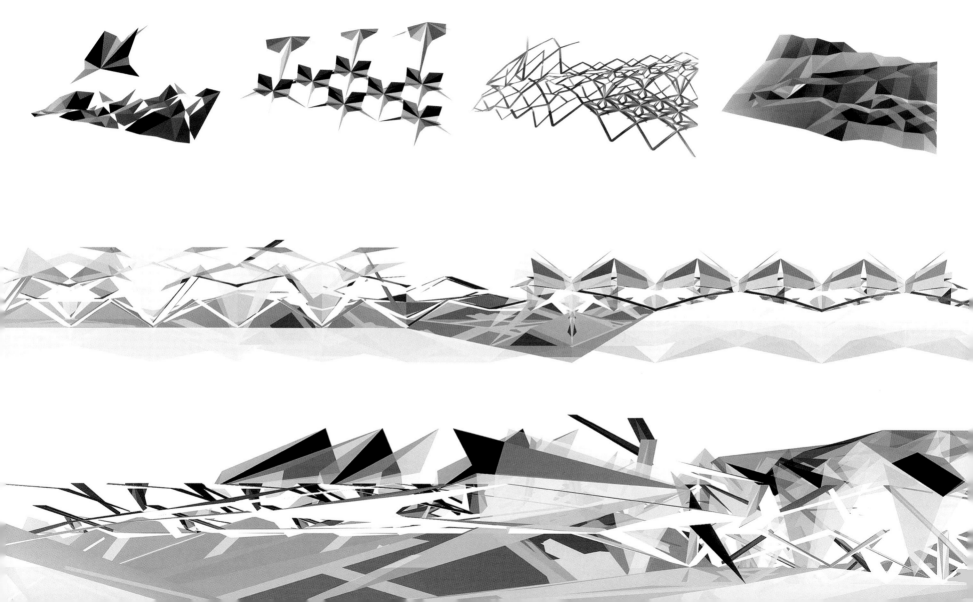

Alejandro Zaera-Polo

On Landscape

The opposition between the rational and the organic that structures the history of landscape design has characterized the history of several disciplines, from philosophy to urbanism. The conflict between a rational, artificial, linear geometry and a picturesque reproduction of nature through less determined geometry permeates the history of landscape. It is in the overcoming of this opposition that we think the possibility of an emerging landscape – and city and architecture – may exist. The emerging landscape will be characterized by developments already occurring in biotechnology, artificial intelligence, design and lifestyle, where the natural and the artificial have become virtually indistinguishable. The mutant, the hybrid and the morphed are likely to replace the machine or Frankenstein as the stereotypes of this century.

The first attempts to manipulate and artificially organize land arose from the need either to exploit or appropriate it, physically and culturally. Both the utilitarian patterns of farming, irrigation and land ownership, and the more cultural and symbolic patterns appearing in monuments and gardens, bear extraordinary similarities to each other across the globe: they are characterized by the deployment of linear, simple geometries – lines, circles, squares, triangles – in stark opposition to chaotic (although we prefer complex) natural organizations, generated through negotiation of multiple orders – geological, biological, climatic – in a morphogenetic process. These simple geometries are the outcome of primitive techniques of land measuring, and are similar across virtually all cultures, from China through Islam, to pre-Columbian America. These types of geometry prevailed with very few exceptions essentially until the eighteenth century, when English landscape designers started using the complex geometries of nature as a source of spatial effects and narratives. However, the geometries of such picturesque gardens were generated through imitation rather than invention, and in that sense they only looked as if they were geometrically complex.

Olmsted invested natural geometry with function, but his geometrical techniques remained basically reproductive and picturesque rather than constructed. Burle Marx invested complex geometries with meaning. Modern parks returned to 'natural' landscape forms, but the discipline never developed a means of producing complexity away from imitation, and never evolved beyond the picturesque. The difficulty of designing complex forms was too much of a disciplinary barrier. In 1968 the modernist hegemony subsided and a general interest in artificial complexity emerged. In architecture, chaos was modelled as a collage, an unmediated relationship between elements and orders that interfere with each other without suffering an erosion of their own identities, instead constructing a new identity through opposition. Postmodernism and deconstruction explored the capacity of this contradictory juxtaposition as the generator of a new order. Simple, artificial orders – circles, lines, grids – were deployed inconsistently on the field, remaining unaffected, unmediated. Regular forms deployed inconsistently or regular programmes deployed in contradiction to each other were the collage techniques that characterized the landscape of the late twentieth century.

The geometries of pure indetermination or pure linearity are a trace of the past rather than a possibility for the future. The opportunity that lies ahead of us is to overcome the disciplinary barrier that resorts to contradiction as a form of complexity (as in *Complexity and Contradiction*), and instead exploit complexity through coherence and consistency. We must learn to produce forms and topographies that are entirely artificial and yet complex, and to generate them through a mediated, integrated addition of rigorous orders. This was the experiment we conducted in Downsview, a shortlisted competition where the objective was to design a Canadian National Park for the twenty-first century. Our intention was to blend the natural and the artificial into a complex organization, neither through arbitrary techniques nor by using the picturesque approach. The proposal was constructed by artificially generating a new topography for the site that would appear as a series of ripples redolent of the glacial formation of the local landscape, a kind of artificial densification. The orders we used to construct these formations incorporated a number of factors. The main ones were the hybridization of water management proposal to purify the drainage water for the park and a topography of circuits for a variety of sports, along with the use of the topography to block the wind. The north-south rippling was no longer derived from a natural dendritic drainage pattern, and yet it was not oblivious to the preexisting topography in its earth-movement strategies. The new topography produced terraces to allow for certain sports to be played, but was also determined by a complex circuit of slopes that followed the gradation of the intensity and density of the different paths – from walking to mountain climbing, from recreational to off-road biking to running paths that replicate the various programmes of a treadmill. This intensification of the circuits produced a gradual differentiation between multiple programmes across the field, aiming towards a topographical consistency between, rather than juxtaposition of, programmes. The new topography was constructed by rolling the section of a natural earth slope around lines of the circuits. The aim was to cease to distinguish between natural and artificial construction. We do not need to resort to the 'pure' artificial forms, to detach geometry from the contingencies of the topography, wind or vegetation; we can adjust them through computer modelling of the forces. Only by applying these techniques rigorously will we be able to meet the challenge of creating a new discipline across the natural and the artificial, the rational and the organic.

landscapeurbanismhappensintime

The competition for Downsview Park in Toronto signals a shift in the design of urban land-scapes, announced most emphatically by the claim of the winning project to be '100% natural and 100% artificial'. All of the projects fold nature and artifice together in ways pertinent not only to landscape design but to urbanism as well, pointing to an interwoven conception of urban–natural systems and morphologies. The Digital and the Coyote, the submission by Bernard Tschumi, Derek Revington and Sterling Finlayson, sets up the distinctions between landscape and city, culture and nature, entertainment and wildness, only to mix them up so that they permeate one another in the fluid production of new landscapes, mediascapes and eventscapes. Brown & Storey's Emergent Landscapes offers a system of coevolving landscapes – thickening and interconnected – which they liken to grammar strings (an oak savannah with a braided network of roads, paths and trails), chunks (activity fields and earthworks) and patches (community and water gardens). Field Operations propose a carefully gauged frame-work for Emergent Ecologies, a matrix of interacting systems that would bring energy, activity and diversity to the site over time, enabling both natural and cultural life to move through and colonize the park in multiple, flexible and emergent ways. Foreign Office Architects, KMPB and Peter Walker propose a New Synthetic Landscape in the fusion of form and flow, reshaping landforms to perform simultaneously for the regeneration of natural systems (water flows, vegetation and habitat) and the cultivation of recreational activities (extreme as well as pastoral). Underscoring the urban implications of collapsing the nature-culture distinction, Koolhaas/Mau/Blaisse/Worland call their project Tree City and emphasize its abstract and diagrammatic character. With a repertoire of geometric elements to be materialized incremen-tally as a thousand meandering pathways and an irregular pattern of circular tree clusters, ponds, wetlands and gathering spaces, Tree City provides a recipe for the park to develop over time, remaining open to shifting desires and opportunities, both social and ecological.

This is hardly the first time that a new union of nature and artifice, landscape and urbanism, has been declared, but the Downsview projects do so under the sign of process, not form, or more precisely, of processes that constitute dynamic systems. From Laugier to Le Corbusier, Haussmann's Paris to picturesque garden cities and modernist Siedlungen, the garden and the landscape have been invoked as formal models with which to reform the city. Dissolving the concentrated mass of the metropolis into a dispersed pattern of buildings set in open landscapes promised a solution to the problematic conditions of modernization in a Utopia of formal integration. As early as the 1920s, the merging of city and nature in a new form of territorial urbanization was evocatively termed *Stadtlandschaft* ('city-landscape') by the German geographer Siegfried Passarge.

In the present era, which FOA/KPMB/PWA have characterized in terms of 'organic prosthetics, biological computers, genetically modified foods, animal cloning and the human genome', the Downsview competitors have taken the collapse of distinction between culture and nature, urban and wild, as a reality, not a Utopian goal. Moreover, they have understood these terms to designate not formal paradigms but subsystems that interact and coevolve, and are guided by dynamic logics that operate across the human-nonhuman divide.

Together, these shifts imply a fundamental rethinking of design from reform to intervention, from projecting visions to stimulating transformations. Form itself is reconceptualized as the result of shaping processes rather than an end in itself. Or more radically stated, form is understood as never fixed but always in flux and susceptible to changing forces. When forms cease to be models, they become tools or devices (lines, circles, ridges, circuits) capable of triggering changes in existing spatial environments and in the life practices that take place within them.

Formally compelling, the Downsview projects are more significant for demonstrating a new conception of design, focusing on practices and techniques that invest matter with intelligence, animation and potential. Reshaping and redirecting, deleting and inserting, seeding and planting, structuring and unstructuring, separating and mixing, mutating and accelerating, are all procedures in landscape design geared towards the production of certain effects while monitoring changes that occur within the environment – changes that are often surprising. The Downsview projects point to the potential benefits of transposing such techniques onto urban design and, conversely, transposing urbanizing procedures – even branding – onto the design of landscapes hitherto presumed to be purely natural.

To realize the benefits of such reciprocity between landscape and urban design, new tools are being developed with which to describe and analyse existing conditions as fully as possible prior to intervening in them. The Downsview competitors map the many facets of the site and its history, but also zoom out to study its role within the larger urban, social, economic and natural contexts, understood as not only systemic but also diachronic phenomena. They marshal a formidable array of analytical frameworks and devices, drawing on modes of analysis developed for urban morphologies, regional ecosystems, transportation and services infrastructure, economic development, cultural geography and marketing. Although the knowledge produced this way is both illuminating and strategic for the development of these design proposals, new techniques of modelling and visualization are still needed to grasp the dynamic relationships between the phenomena that these perspectives seek to describe. Are there better tools for describing and analysing phenomena across the urban-natural divide? Can the methods of ecosystem analysis be merged with those of urban form, infrastructure and development? How can change over time be studied better in relation to the interaction of generative forces? How are the effects of change to be assessed?

The emphasis on temporality and transformation in the Downsview projects comes in part from landscape design, which has long understood its medium – nature – to be simultaneously dynamic and systemic, and open to interventions that alter the entire system. But in part it also comes from complexity theory, which does not draw rigid distinctions between natural and social phenomena and has been used to explain self-organizing behaviour in everything from slim moulds and ant colonies to human economies and cities. As the science writer Steven Johnson explains in *Emergence: The Connected Lives of Ants, Brains, Cities, and Software* (2001), the study of self-organization has developed over the past 30 years as scientists have struggled to understand the phenomenon of emergence in complex adaptive systems in which there is no single regulatory or guiding authority. Without higher-level instructions, following only local and nonhierarchical protocols, such systems produce

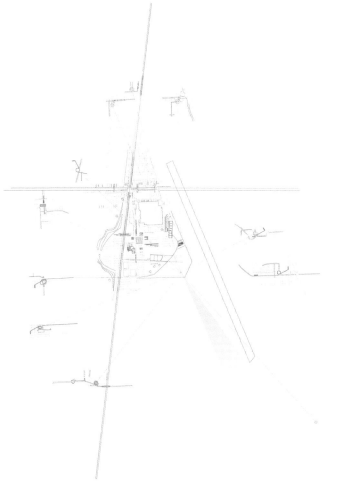

Brown & Storey Architects, Emergent Landscapes

discernible macrobehaviour through the dynamic interaction of multiple agents in multiple ways. Johnson draws parallels between such emergent, or seemingly unplanned, behaviours in both organic and urban systems by citing Lewis Mumford's animated descriptions of medieval European cities and Jane Jacobs' account of the social and economic dynamics of Greenwich Village in the 1950s. More recently, self-organizing systems have been built into software, video games, art and music, generating artificial systems that exploit the laws of emergence. 'Up to now', Johnson declares, 'the philosophers of emergence have struggled to interpret the world. But they are now starting to change it'. How can the new sciences of complexity provide more-effective approaches to understanding and operating within the dynamic systems of the natural/built environment, systems in which adaptability is becoming increasingly important?

While time began to be inscribed in science and art in the late-nineteenth and early-twentieth centuries, its integration into modern architecture and urbanism remained limited, although movement came to play a larger role. When time did enter in, it tended to appear in the reductive form of linear causality, functional equilibrium or the play of dialectics. Russian disurbanist linear cities, Le Corbusier's Radiant City and Ludwig Hilberseimer's Settlement Units conceived of urban dynamics in rudimentary ways: they incorporated growth, extension and movement along structured lines, but not the formative dynamics of economy, politics and society. Hilberseimer's proposed mutation of a district in Chicago into a city-landscape was a rare instance of thinking about urban morphology transforming over time. Yet by envisioning the final result in advance, the process could only implement a fixed schema. Notwithstanding the propensity of architects for borrowing metaphors from biology, the conception of nature in modernist urban visions remained untouched by the dynamics of morphology, evolution and ecology, let alone those of morphogenesis and self-organization. Even Hilberseimer, concerned that poor agricultural practices were leading to soil erosion, treated nature in his projects as little more than a green pattern.

On the other hand, modernist urban histories of the mid-century – such as Mumford's *The Culture of Cities* (1938), Sigfried Giedion's *Space, Time, and Architecture* (1941) and Hilberseimer's *The Nature of Cities* (1955) – were more alive to formative dynamics. They portrayed urban morphologies as collective constructs in time, constantly changing in relation to historical events and the interaction of shaping forces. In animated prose, these writers depicted the

Field Operations, Emergent Ecologies, this page and opposite

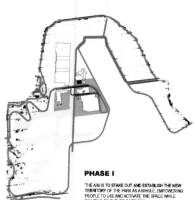

PHASE I

THE AIM IS TO STAKE OUT AND ESTABLISH THE NEW
TERRITORY OF THE PARK AS A WHOLE, EMPOWERING
PEOPLE TO USE AND ACTIVATE THE SPACE WHILE
POINTING TO FUTURE POTENTIAL

EARTHWORKS
PERIMETER PLANTING
SURFACING
MEDIA MALL + PLAZA

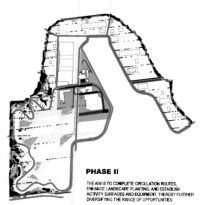

PHASE II

THE AIM IS TO COMPLETE CIRCULATION ROUTES,
ENHANCE LANDSCAPE PLANTING, AND ESTABLISH
ACTIVITY SURFACES AND EQUIPMENT, THEREBY FURTHER
DIVERSIFYING THE RANGE OF OPPORTUNITIES

PLANTING II
SURFACING II
CIRCULATION
EQUIPPING
CIRCUIT INFILL I
COVERED AMPITHEATER

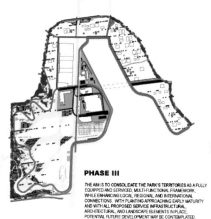

PHASE III

THE AIM IS TO CONSOLIDATE THE PARK'S TERRITORIES AS A FULLY
EQUIPPED AND SERVICED, MULTI-FUNCTIONAL FRAMEWORK,
WHILE ENHANCING LOCAL, REGIONAL, AND INTERNATIONAL
CONNECTIONS. WITH PLANTING APPROACHING EARLY MATURITY
AND WITH ALL PROPOSED SERVICE INFRASTRUCTURAL,
ARCHITECTURAL, AND LANDSCAPE ELEMENTS IN PLACE,
POTENTIAL FUTURE DEVELOPMENT MAY BE CONTEMPLATED.

ROOF STRUCTURES AND OUTDOOR THEATER WITH STAGE
POTENTIAL CIRCUIT INFILL II
SPECIAL FEATURES/EQUIPMENT/FACILITIES
POTENTIAL TUNNEL
POTENTIAL CONVERSION OF SUPPLY DEPOT TO INTERNATIONAL ART VENUE

LONG-TERM POTENTIAL

THE NATURAL SYSTEMS OF THE SITE WILL CONTINUE
TO MATURE AND DIVERSIFY, WHILE THE ARRAY OF
CULTURAL PROGRAMS MAY BE ADDED TO, OR
SUBTRACTED ACCORDING TO CHANGING NEEDS AND
DESIRES. IF THE RUNWAY WERE TO CLOSE AND
BECOME PART OF THE PARK TERRITORY, NEW
EXPANSES OF OPEN SPACE WOULD BECOME
AVAILABLE - VAST PLAINS OR FLOW SPACE
EMBRACED BY NEW ACTIVITY CIRCUITS, AND
OVERLOOKED BY THE BUILDINGS OF THE
DEVELOPMENT PARCELS TO THE NORTH AND EAST.

139

2001   2005   2010   2015   2020

drama of cities rising, falling and transforming in tandem with the fate of empires; the invention of new technologies; changes in society, economic relations and political structures; and new ideas, symbolic forms and ways of living. Their narratives even incorporated cataclysmic forms of change wrought by disease, drought, famine, war and revolution. For them, the present was simply the latest moment in the ongoing mutation of urban form, which architects and urbanists attempted to harness for the sake of new formal paradigms. Mumford's idea that historical eras could be characterized in terms of complexes – either technological complexes of dominant materials, energy and systems of production or social complexes of economic, political and institutional frameworks – provided a powerful tool with which to understand the interaction of formative conditions. However, the idea of the complex had a certain bias towards equilibrium, synthesis and integration, which also made itself manifest in Mumford's dream that garden cities and regional planning would provide a balanced, stable and harmonious urban order for what he called the new biotechnic era.

If landscape urbanism is to breach the human-natural divide, it will need both new descriptive and analytical tools and new kinds of historical models addressing the relationship of urban form and flow to natural systems both within cities and beyond. Manuel de Landa has made the point that, with complexity theory, science has acquired an even greater historical consciousness than it had in the early twentieth century. As he explains, 'All structures that form our reality (mountains, animals and plants, human languages and social institutions) are the products of specific historical processes.' His book A Thousand Years of Non-Linear History (1997) demonstrates the potential of a new kind of historiography that portrays the interwovenness of human and natural ecologies in all its complexity. While drawing on earlier histories such as Mumford's (as Johnson also does), de Landa rejects their bias towards control and comprehensive order, instead understanding the history of structures to be nonlinear, unbalanced, contingent and unpredictable. His sweeping time frame registers patterns and shifts that have occurred over many generations, and his ambitious scope plots the interplay of different populations of life (human, animal, mineral and vegetable). Yet he insists that systematicness should not be postulated in advance of adequate evidence of system-generating processes. Rather he looks at subsets of social systems and works from the bottom up.

Focusing on the much tighter time frame of mid-century America, Keller Easterling's

Organization Space (1999) likewise explores the potential of ecological and network thinking, concentrating on the organization of territories such as landscape systems, highways and housing subdivisions. Venturing into the generic spaces of urbanizing infrastructure and commercial development, Easterling redefines architecture in organizational terms as protocols for formatting space, operational logics that are affected by time and patterns of connectivity. She treats sites as sets of interdependent parts within which even small shifts have enormous effects. Though she eschews any claims to have written a history of architecture or planning, her 'eccentric episodes' (at times even demonstrating the idiosyncrasies of systems) are eminently suggestive for historical studies and are timely reminders of the limitations of totalizing narratives.

In their own ways, Johnson, de Landa and Easterling help us imagine the orientation, scope and modalities of a range of historical studies – studies of practices as much as behaviours – that are needed to inform the new modes of design now emerging in the rich territory of 'landscapeurbanism'.

CONTEXT ▸

Avoiding the simple opposition between environmental and developmental logics, landscape urbanism increases natural resilience by artificially breeding new organizational capabilities to host the coexistence and coevolution of the some of the most diversified and dynamic ecologies and economies, integrating the fastest processes of development with the highest levels of environmental stress. Beyond mere sustainability, landscape urbanism makes use of the intensity and urgency of these ecologies and economies through the enhancement and escalation of natural systems in complex pieces of infrastructure. The landscape embodies the ultimate opportunity to intermingle systems in a consistent cybernetic universe, a machine with its own laws. The machinic landscape is pure exteriority evolving, where the natural absorbs the social and where the systemic absorbs the linguistic. It explodes the sedimented structure of the social and offers the aggressive reality of the systemic that largely overwhelms it, disbelieving naturalistic urban realities and overriding artificial natures. Its fertility resides in its capacity for unfolding the urban towards extreme scenarios. The landscape grounds innovation without succumbing to the critical. It sharply breaks the conventions of urbanism through redundancy. In this context, landscape urbanism is theory without representation and practice without teleology.–CN

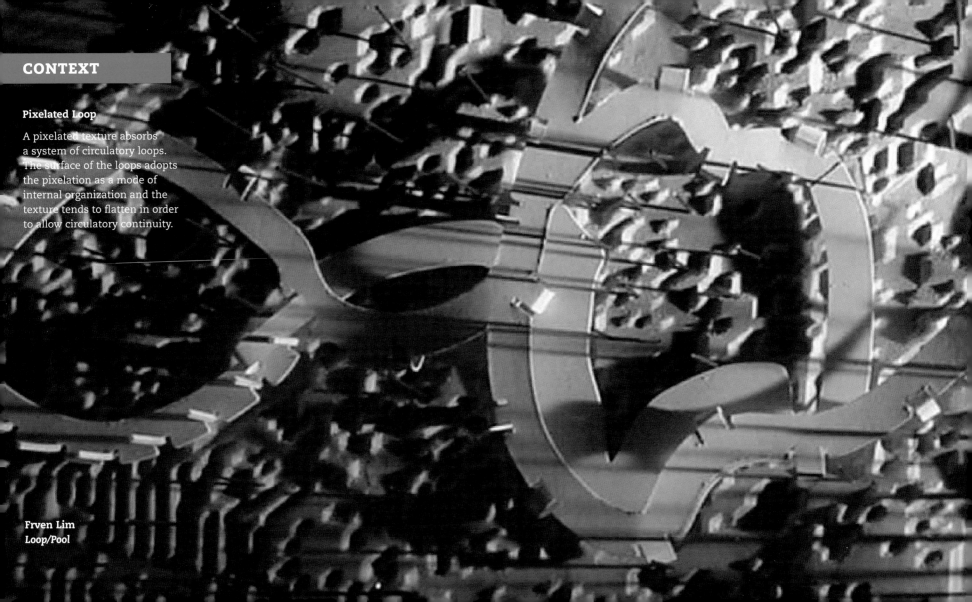

Pixelated Loop

A pixelated texture absorbs
a system of circulatory loops.
The surface of the loops adopts
the pixelation as a mode of
internal organization and the
texture tends to flatten in order
to allow circulatory continuity.

Frven Lim
Loop/Pool

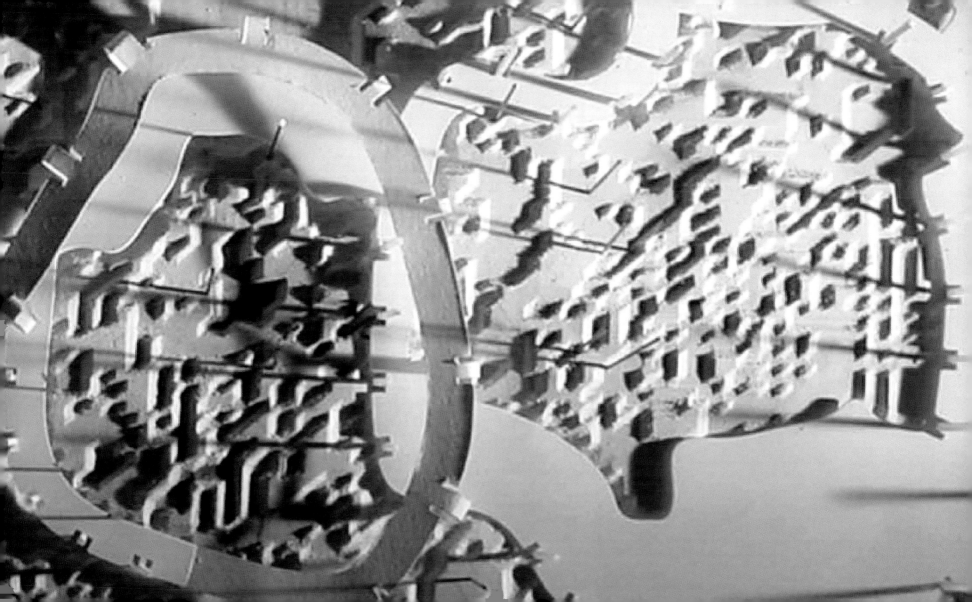

Bundled Archipelago

Shops are described as linear protocols working in series. They are made continuous in order to constitute circulatory bundles, follow the road pattern and configure medium-size shopping islands, which remain in a state of semi-open seclusion.

Simona Bencini
Windowscape

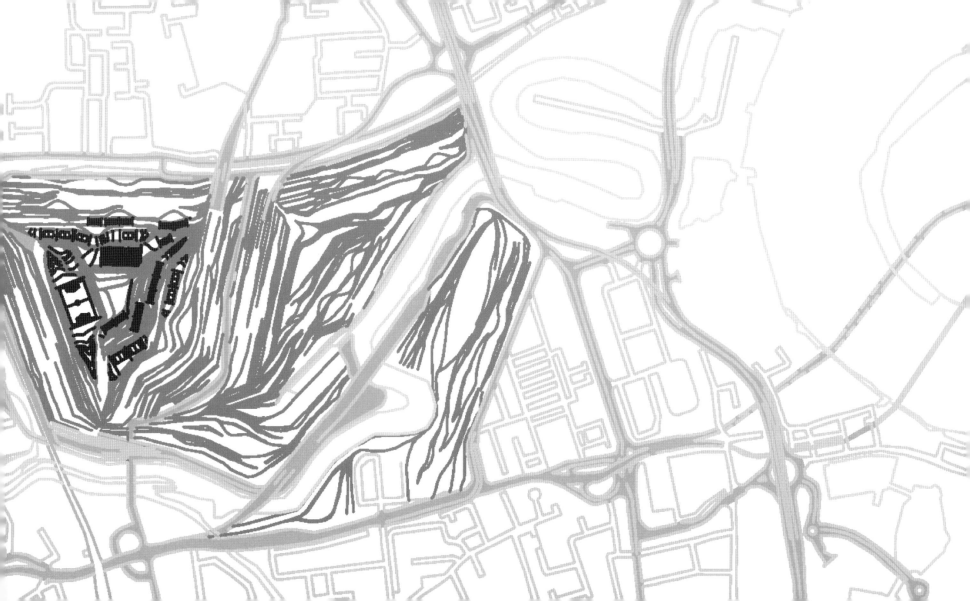

Adaptive Grid

A space-frame structure, a circulatory mesh and a system of plantation bands are integrated in an adaptive grid that regulates developmental modules.

Santiago Bozzola
Changing Structures

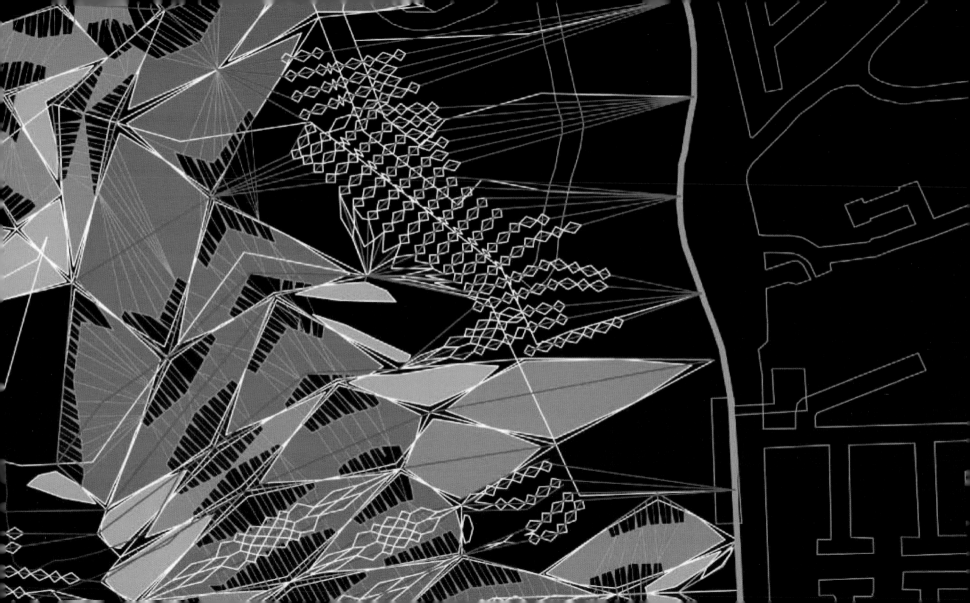

Field Transformation

The decontamination of the
land is achieved through
excavation and selective
displacement, construction of
raw infrastructure and
regulation of programmatic
settlements, configuring a
mechanism of transformation
and resistance to future
developments.

Julia Wessendorf
Leisure Masses

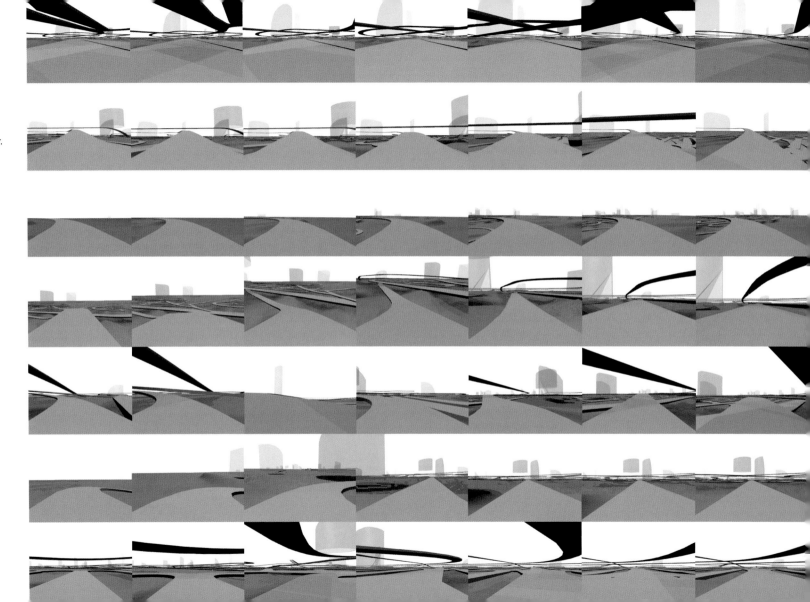

Vectorial Unfolding

Developmental envelopes result from a dynamic curatorial mechanism that unfolds the vehicular circulation onto the territory. Animation tests.

Jose Parral
Artland

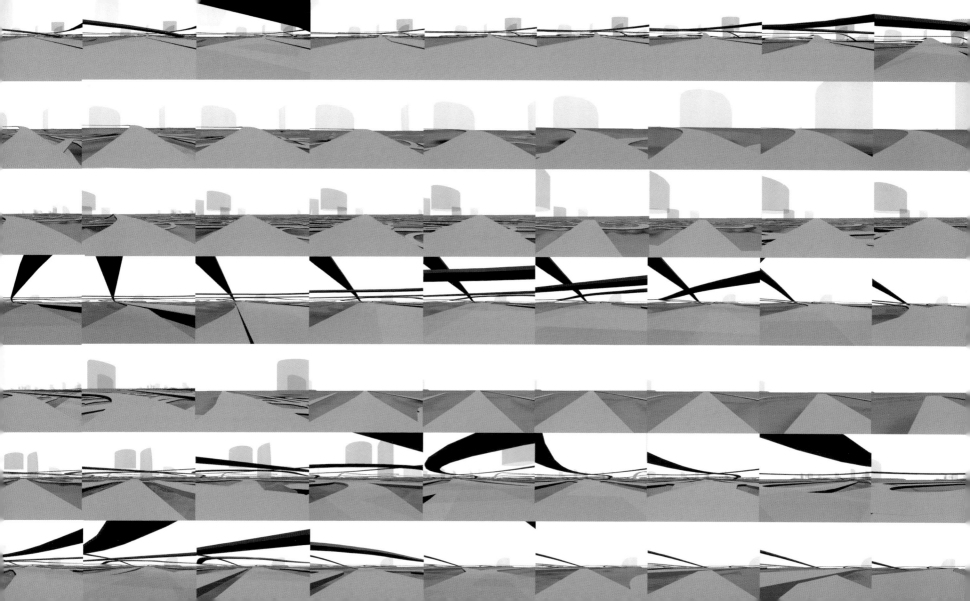

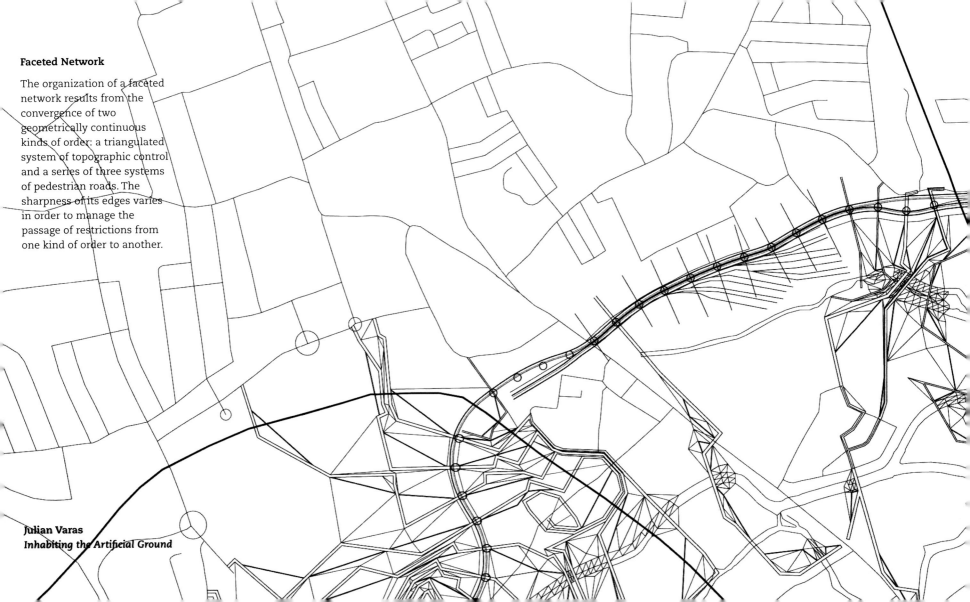

Faceted Network

The organization of a faceted network results from the convergence of two geometrically continuous kinds of order: a triangulated system of topographic control and a series of three systems of pedestrian roads. The sharpness of its edges varies in order to manage the passage of restrictions from one kind of order to another.

Julian Varas
Inhabiting the Artificial Ground

Error

For so many strata of culture – from geology to network architecture to urbanism and globalization – landscape is diagram. Like a diagram, it requires no representation. Like a diagram, it has temporal parameters. Like a diagram, it is not reliant on any single artefact but rather continues to produce artefacts in time. It is an organization that is always becoming.

While landscape presents the impossibility of representation by any default convention such as contour or pictorial frame, it often meets this default impulse in culture. Landscape is useful in the sense that in the history of its associations it has acquired markers for two divergent meanings: *landskip*, referencing a pictorial or framed landscape, and *landschaaf*, a farmed landscape that is not represented but is rather worked and conditioned. *Landschaaf* would then describe agriculture rather than scenery. It frames a set of tasks and sites that are concerned not with the aesthetics of the whole but with the reconditioning of a field by means of adjustments. Repetition may amplify these adjustments, and inventions may join the genetics of the crop in purposeful but not entirely predictable ways.

An expansive contemplation of landscape often already associates with other models of active organization, from, for instance, genetics, epidemiology, earth sciences, networks or logistical theatres. Each of these active organizations also stumbles over its default representations in culture. Figural evocations of the body often mask systemic understanding. A common notation for a working urban landscape merges landscape, terrain or domain with network habits for designating related points or values in a field as topological space. This topological space, as it is compatible with geometric representations, often masks an understanding of network behaviours and, more importantly, the values of information itself, since the topology is not the information, the information is the information. For many, digital devices are simply a new set of interfaces, switches and capabilities in the larger colloidal field of everything else, and so they are about the landscapes within which they are embedded: our bodies, our larger marketplaces and networks, and our daily theatres of operation. Yet as these tools facilitate the making of complex geometries, they also prompt a rather conservative initial use in architecture culture, perhaps even a self-parody of the twentieth-century architect. Posing as the modest cybernetician with the tousled hair, the architect, though talking about unknowable complexity, wants more than anything to predict or represent the forms and formats of an unknowable web of connections. Scripts from science fiction, complexity theory, neobiological organums, technocracy or futurology fuel a secret ego for questing unifying theories, recursive organizations and holism all within the gigantic fiction that information is successive rather than coexistent. Whether the geometry is Euclidean or epigenetic, the approach is a conservative early rehearsal.

Any of the organizations that currently inform landscape, from genetics to networks, offer intelligence about multiples: multiples that need not always resolve themselves into a whole, the more diverse, messy and redundant the better. New information in the form of error, accident and redundancy strengthens organization. Continuity does not necessarily describe a condition of total connectedness but the power of partial connectedness, overlap and amplification of effect in a population of things. Popular fascinations with complexity theories often frame a world of data territories within which a predictable principle emerges, a world with its own periodicity and catastrophe. While we are currently fond of a kind of this spectacular-but-determinate notion of chaos, we might look instead for truly extensive information – foreign territory, resistance, discontinuities and unpatterned multiples. Perhaps the more productive search is not for homeostasis but for the inexplicable and even cruel ecologies in organizations that are continually exiting themselves.

This intelligence radicalizes a contemplation of site, that part of speech that in architecture is always singular, but that in landscape, network or any other active organization is always plural. It is a multiple condition within which the partial or the remote is empowered to deflect a population. The focus is not on the topological space that resolves the information into a single entity, but on the diverse points of information themselves, information that is not cloaked in geometrical skins. The adjusters, the toggles of the field, are manifold. They are the multiple sites, the population whose larger field cannot be framed. Site in this sense is difficult to pursue with the hierarchical sequence of architectural drawing convention, moving stepwise from masterplan to building and construction detail. Site might instead exist in a repertoire, one requiring all of the discipline's well-rehearsed skills of measure and explicit instruction but applicable to multiple conditions with not entirely predictable effect. This combination of repertoire and scenario is itself a more robust structure, a diagram with more potential responses.

Error is a good marker for the sites in a population. After all, a study of error is a study of organization. If error makes organizations robust, perhaps it is more constantly and abundantly present in a world that attempts to foreground the stability, unity and recursivity that it does not have. Every significant invention is surrounded not by sensible thinking but by imagination and fiction, eccentricity and error. Error sometimes operates like comedy, in the sense that it can topple constructs. It refocuses attention on site that is now multiplied at the atomized condition, the network of remotes that derive power from being only partially continuous, or part of many continuities.

A field guide to this landscape, to this atomized condition, like the books that rehearse strategies in chess or *tsugis* in go, would operate like a playbook of error. Error is the kind of event that, like snow, requires 200 descriptors or modifiers. Error includes exception, mistake and accident, but also trick, wild card, category mistake and joke. Error also includes artistic tricks, *perruques*, *détournement* and reversal. Some entries would footnote Ryle, Huizinga, Bakhtin, de Certeau or Debord. But the entries would also include species of error that are gigantic, central, powerful versions of these disguises and tricks, and that are somewhere on a continuum between tactic and strategy.

When architecture makes its own world of data territories, it excludes the wide world that really is made of data territories and networks, a world where space is poised to play a pivotal role in global politics, and where the invention of spatial components can leverage organizations of labour, natural resources and patterns of consumption. Since landscape often serves as an appropriate diagram for some of these conditions, it refracts through many strata of information in culture and so expands the fields of architectural influence towards other operations and organizational logics that accompany not just the space of geometries and building envelopes but larger fields of deployment. This responsibility, real and thrilling, emerges as an architectural project.

-scape has become a suffix for a strata of global influence in culture, whether associated with fashion, commerce or politics. For instance, Arjun Appadurai's five culturalscapes – ethnoscapes, mediascapes, technoscapes, financescapes and ideoscapes – help model a condition of globalization space, multiple and conflicting influences that must always be partial and overlapping. While these landscapes are 'inflected by the historical, linguistic and political situatedness of different sorts of actors: nation-states, multinational, diasporic communities, as well as subnational groupings and movements (whether religious, political or economic), and even intimate face-to-face groups, such as villages, neighbourhoods and families', individual agents are the sources of some constant reconditioning. The *-scapes* are also mobile, almost fluvial, and so counter the argument model of globalization as a homogenizing steamroller of forces. Similarly, Manuel de Landa returns to ideas their literal as well as diagrammatic geology. He traces the 'lavas' and 'magmas' in a history of urban development, relating natural resources to cultural groups and urban technologies.

The sea is another landscape diagram that has captured the imagination of contemporary cultural theorists. For Deleuze, the sea perfectly diagrams multiplicity and differential repetition. It is suggestive of 'a single and same Ocean for all the drops', but only when each drop has reached an 'excess', an 'extremity of difference' – '… the difference which displaces and disguises them and, in turning upon its mobile cusp, causes them to return'. In a political sea that is perhaps not so perfectly anarchical, as in de Certeau, the force of collective tactics can, as he describes, flood or recede against the islands of official power. Deleuzian political philosophers Hardt and Negri also model the collective multitude as a sea of political power, an ocean of globalization that is uncontrollable but navigable, and not, by virtue of its ubiquity, simply benign. Since navigating the sea requires slipping through jurisdictions and shifting disguises, it beautifully models the transnational network of flows. The sea continues to shape a substrate of urbanism while also growing urbanism in the form of new fields of global transshipment and of new migrations of labour.

Global 'orgmen' manipulate scapes constructed of data territories. The orgman is at once a comedian – funniest in his most earnest moments – and a pirate on the sea of globalization.

He believes himself to be literally producing space from time and desire. The generic software and hardware formats, the 'real-estate products' for offices, malls, entertainment centres, theatres and other programmes, form new conglomerates or merge with museums and amusements as various critical paths in streamlining consumption are adopted and discarded. Though the orgman uses his formats to alter millions of square feet around the globe, his supposedly optimized logistics are always on the verge of being replaced and always subject to the comedies of the marketplace – a marketplace based not on inherent values or logic, but rather reliant on consumer desires that are created and ignored. The orgman is a great manipulator of error and differential value. Error may not be the exception to our industry, but rather the only thing we produce – a solid crop of errors, remainders and resold merchandise at accident prices. The orgman's world operates in ways that are elaborate and strange, hilarious and full of temporary public space. It is a world that relies on mistakes, risks and exceptional desires to make it not banal and monolithic but penetrable.

Although landscape borrows and loans intelligence from new paradigms about complex organization, some of the earliest landscape theorists, scientists and polymaths are strangely compatible with contemporary theories. This early work appeared before the more pious and emotional scripts of conservation, and at the moment when earth sciences were shifting from cataloguing artefacts to articulating expressions of landscape movement over time. Two such thinkers provide examples. Thomas Henry Huxley borrowed the term 'physiography' from mineralogy, using it to describe landscape in action. His narrative of landscape urbanism by the same name applied this thinking to a temporal study of the Thames Basin, relating the characteristics of the region to the changing effects of tides and atmospheric conditions, and describing the urban 'flows' of commerce through history in terms of a fluvial model. Benton MacKaye, an American landscape theorist influenced by Huxley, also used fluvial models, describing flows of commerce, labour and natural resources in gigantic American sites organized around highways, waterways and other mediating lines, not only on the North American continent but in a transnational network of exchange. Both manipulated an interplay between the technologies of urbanism and the forces of landscape. MacKaye even described the urban landscape as a kind of wilderness, a landscape of technologies as yet unexplored.

'Terra incognita', another of MacKaye's terms to describe this wilderness, is useful in exploring the sea of global urbanization, the territories of the orgman, of tourism, of trans-shipment or of labour migrations. The sites are mobile, sometimes only appearing as a set of instructions that repeatedly format large areas of land. In a global exchange that establishes its military and political fronts on economic rather than ideological lines, change will continue to rely on ingenuity with natural resources (e.g., oil, water, timber, minerals and natural gas) and alternative technologies. These changes may not square up to political ideas directly either with warfare or a heroic, principled stance, but rather leverage an avalanche of change with an invention that indirectly alters the ambient chemistry of persuasions about consumption and landscape. These remotes might be discovered or produced by researching site in terra incognita – a broad and discontinuous terrain for the excesses of design.

Ciro Najle

Convolutedness*

Under the assumption that architectural determination and its false opposition to indeterminacy must be reconsidered in a context where no future actuality can be definitively predicted, the following essay attempts to contribute to a theory of the actual, considered as a momentary state in a consistent evolutionary process that proceeds by differentiation. It is a contribution to a theory of material production, considered as a deviation from within this process. It is an attempt to construct a systematic approximation of this deviation, with an insinuation of an emergent relationship between practice and theory through the engineering of new modes of practice. This project requires the consideration of history as a construction that operates within expansive and fluctuating temporalities, beyond the social. It also involves the consideration of technology as a meta-ideological project and at the same time as a historically determined construction. And it assumes as its condition of existence the radical transformation of hard sciences after cybernetics and during their massive engagement with complexity, which it adopts as a model of thought. Finally, this essay follows and feeds a cultural project that attempts the double dissolution of the architectural object and the architect-hero, which is incarnated by the opening of the discipline to the larger realms of the urban and the landscape.

The notion of convolutedness is the by-product of several genealogies, some vague, some literal. In part it carries the notion of senselessness as the condition for a purely circumstantial operativity, without grounding and without the need for grounding. It also refers to evolution as it coils around itself. Further, convolutedness is a formal category meaning voluptuousness, and it represents the attempt to construct a paradigm that mixes pragmatics and beauty through exuberance and redundancy. It also appeals for abundance: abundant agents under play, abundant material involved, abundant operations performed, abundant varieties engendered. And most obviously, convolutedness refers to turbulent flow (volvo: turn), trying to collaborate in the incorporation into the disciplinary jargon of new devices with which to think dynamically about order and control. Finally, its reference to 'volutas' also suggests affinities, for which it makes no direct claims.

*The essay was developed as a derivation of problems initially formulated by Rem Koolhaas in 'Bigness'. The notion of convolutedness tangentially brings a qualitative, time-based and process-orientated condition into the quantitative, type-based and object-orientated condition of bigness, which it follows and recalls. OMA, Rem Koolhaas and Bruce Mau, S,M,L,XL (Monacelli Press: 1995), pp. 495–516.

... or else, the physics of vortices, of sweetness, and of smiling voluptuousness.
MICHEL SERRES, 1982[1]

Beyond certain velocities, architecture acquires the voluptuous properties and the abundant regime of 'convolutedness': a serene state of continuous agitation. By increasing its speed, a system multiplies its interactions and is compelled to open up and behave smoothly. The best reason to broach convolutedness is that 'a laminar flow is nothing else than ideal and theoretical'.[2] Convolutedness is the ubiquitous condition of architecture: uniqueness engineered by the proliferation of vitality. It seems incredible that the speed of the processes involved in a development performs a nonideological unfolding, a desire independent yet inclusive of the will of the architects. It seems even harder to accept that this unfolding does not carry a rationale, although it carries a consistency that is chaotic without being aleatory. Of all possible categories, convolutedness does not seem to deserve a manifesto: discredited in principle by mechanicism, it was imprisoned as an accident in the spatial continuum, like a 'calamitous monstrosity'. But in fact, only convolutedness incarnates and instigates the regime of complexity that forces the emergence of an integrative intelligence where architecture participates and potentially commands.

After the Second World War, a generation of scientific breakthroughs and technological developments triggered a synthetic evolution of materials that had been developing since the Industrial Revolution, to the point of producing a new evolutionary leap. This process unleashed a series of hidden material evolutions and 'shameful' architectural convolutions that became culturally visible through several *tardo*-surrealist operations, retrospective manifestos, intriguing trips to the unknown, semantic apparatuses, and operative classifications, in the context of a foreign-orientated ethos and a tortuous, slippery humour.

By introducing new technologies and by proliferating their infrastructure, by intensively increasing, redistributing or spreading their envelopes, by stretching and shrinking the depth-to-perimeter ratio, by complexifying their internal organization and incorporating extraneous organizational logics, by redefining their components and introducing new relationships, by making more sophisticated their media manoeuvres and inventing and appropriating new modes of communication and transfer of information, by gradually overwriting knowledge

1 Michel Serres, *Hermes: Literature, Science Philosophy* (Johns Hopkins University Press: 1982), p. 101.
2 Michel Serres, *The Birth of Physics* (Clinamen Press Ltd.: 2001), p. 23.

with knowledge, the dynamics of economic expansion at all scales dissolved any former residue of a political content in the compulsive actualizations of fast systemic developments. The contemporary city became an experimental tableau where the fluctuations of a volatile rationale achieved extremes of creativity through an intense typological redefinition.

No matter how environmentally friendly, politically correct, socially appropriate or economically efficient they appeared at low speeds, the various modes of technological and infrastructural development incarnated lineages of material evolution determined by wide and unpredictable ecologies. These lines became more visible than the objects they themselves produced: increasingly cheap, light and ephemeral, microscopic and disposable, they vanished in front of our eyes, melting into the rapid winds of technology. Segregated domains of production and established ideological apparatuses were deterritorialized by the escalating agility of this collective skill. These lineages, in turn, accelerated the coevolution of wider organizational transformations and the enrichment of the social world, yet not necessarily its progress.

But is it enough to describe this condition as contemporary? Is it simply dependent on a reduced version of historical circumstance? Can this process be captured by the rhythm of a merely human history? Or is it instead constructing a becoming of its own, meta-historical and capable of transforming history as we know it? Moreover: was not this type of duration already there, before our present awareness, and immanent in the prearchitectural tableau of any practice? Acceleration seems to have increased the visibility of the processes of urban transformation, introducing both the possibility of and need for new forms of materialism to understand them. Acceleration seems to have forced them to share a duration similar to our own, enabling our own duration to jump into them without the help of ancillary theoretical devices, without the backup of any illusion. In this altogether new context, the historical relevance of a practice or its contemporaneity cannot prevail anymore as the self-evident basis of its ethos, because it is indeed a multiplicity of ethos that these processes continuously invent: emergent modes of material life. Rather than one of legitimacy, the question turns into the kind of 'becoming' that a practice is producing or how its built-in mechanisms of differ-entiation operate in vaster processes. The question develops into how and how much a practice accelerates or slows its environment, how and how much it enriches itself in this process, how tightly it operates, how fragile it is. We are confronted with a completely different kind of problem. What are the characteristics of the internal regime of a practice? What are its parameters, its ranges and its modes? What are its learning capabilities? How does it absorb change? As to where exactly a practice is leading, it is doubtful whether there will be a definitive answer. In these conditions, there is no external aim, no predictable performance and no 'ultimate' architecture.

The Machinic Landscape

… that mere purposive rationality unaided by such phenomena as art, religion, and the like, is necessarily pathogenic and destructive of life; and that its virulence springs specifically from the circumstance that life depends upon interlocking circuits of contingency, while consciousness can see only such circuits as human purpose may direct…. That is the sort of world we live in – a world of circuit structures – and love can survive only if wisdom (i.e., a sense of recognition of the fact of circuitry) has an effective voice…. But if art, as suggested above, has a positive function in maintaining what I called 'wisdom', i.e., in correcting a too purposive view of life and making the view more systemic, then the question to be asked of the given work of art becomes: what sorts of correction in the direction of wisdom would be achieved by creating or viewing this work of art? The question becomes dynamic rather than static.

GREGORY BATESON, 2000[3]

Trapped between teleology and immateriality, thus rendered rigid and idealistic, and finally sidelined by the increasing speed of urban development, the first generation of late-capitalist architectural and urban practices were constrained by the poverty of the technical capabilities of the discipline in relation to the richness of the processes with which they had to cope. Adjustments in their material palettes, tastes, techniques and strategies often failed to recognize the demand for a qualitative change in their modes of production. The landscape was initially absorbed in this context. It offered the thematic and scalar opportunity to redefine urban problems and the practice in general, incorporating in its operativity a direct engagement with the multiple systems of forces that constantly reconfigure the city. It recontextualized the practice. It introduced immensity: a context so large that urban

3 Gregory Bateson, *Steps to an Ecology of Mind* (University of Chicago Press: 2000), pp. 146–7.

complexity is made simple. It introduced fluctuation: a context of management of contingencies through escalating complexity. It introduced temporality: a context based on nonphysical determinations. It introduced interactivity: a context with a life of its own. And it introduced simultaneity: a context of integration of disparate simultaneous conditions. These contexts offered the conditions for a different perception of temporal developments.

Based on the recognition of these new logics, but in the attempt to go beyond the mere understanding, collection, composition and redeployment of their organizational effects, the practices of the second generation set up the task of engineering new operative capacities through the exploration of new techniques of organization. These techniques were foreign to the representational apparatus in which the discipline had locked itself, and discontinuous with its traditional conventions. This discontinuity was initially traversed through metaphoric leaps, hybridizations, conceptualizations, misunderstandings or simple vagueness. There was a lack of a medium that could receive and handle a continuity across domains of production.

This medium acquires consistency all at once, through the expansion of mechanistic ethos into the machinic. The five contexts that the landscape provides are operatively integrated into the five aspects of the machinic: multiscalarity, transspecificity, prephysicality, performativity and internal coexistence. Multiscalarity provides the conditions to surpass the extra-large as a condition for the emergence of complexity. Transspecificity circumvents the need for discrimination of domains in order to handle complexity. Prephysicality delays the physical in a temporality in which complexity is processed. Intensivity constitutes the condition for the interactivity of this medium. Virtual coexistence provides concrete conditions for managing simultaneity. These five aspects are integrated into a multiplicitous system of causal relations working in circuits. They build up, with systematic specificity, the armature to hold together disparate cultural, economic, social and environmental processes. They constitute a technically precise, consistent and complex virtuality. The landscape is thus abstracted into the machinic by becoming a simulation: a virtual material field that operates as the preurbanism of urbanism, an immanent, dynamic, deterritorializing land. Across scales, the machinic landscape works as a field of computation that mediates between domains and integrates tendencies, desires and demands, fostering organizational interactions and segregations, consolidations and destabilizations.

This meta-infrastructure of negotiation involves processes of propagation in two simultaneous directions, and the engineering of the actualization of their potentials: in one direction it intensifies virtual potentials through their progressive specification; in the other, it integrates disparate informational realms into a single organizational system. Each direction corresponds to the two simultaneous and opposite tendencies of a simple movement of actualization. They revolve onto each other in convolution.

Virtual Megalomania

Cybernetics was the name given to the literally symbiotic art of steering and
governing by loops, loops engendered by these angles and that engender, in turn,
other directional angles.
MICHEL SERRES, 1995[4]

Convolutedness develops from the iterative looping of lines of differentiation back into themselves in a synergistic medium. On the one hand, flows of information cascade in a multiple sequence of cause and effect. A function-matter vector is profiled and regulated through development scenarios, benefit charts, management tools and user catalogues. At the same time, material primitives unfold potentials in order to index performances in a consistent regime. Norms and codifications, local habits, cultural jargons, structural limits and construction technologies absorb and constrain contingencies. The simultaneity of these two directions is solved by an increasingly fertile fluctuation. Processes of propagation and selection in both directions amplify and steer the evolving circuitry of relations. They progressively distribute and coordinate forces. They mesh them in networks of increasing complexity. They merge them with the territory. By generating, testing, selecting and regenerating variants, the circuitry accumulatively breeds proto-organizations with infrastructural capabilities. It works as a technological augmentation of natural resilience. It intensifies and expands performance. It idealizes. The evolving organizations constitute overspecific generalities: while retaining and sustaining a high degree of openness in their virtual potentials, they integrate multiple lines of differentiation. Beyond certain thresholds, the organizations merge with the circuit, acquire their own force and forecast themselves.

165

4 Michel Serres, *The Natural Contract* (University of Michigan Press: 1995), p. 42.

In this context, the development, planning, implementation and construction of a material organization can be said to operate as a system with no programme, but an increasingly complex diagram. Its frameworks are continually provisional. Its boundaries are open. All finalities are engulfed and dissolved, and control is distributed into multiplicitous power relations. Determination is thus reconfigured and adjusted in an artificially constructed environment of production: folded energy that unfolds in a consistent medium. A machinic practice achieves sheer operativity, without degrading into plain technique. By its own fluctuation it becomes a mode of embedment. An apparently paradoxical megalomania emerges out of this process of intense determination: where a programme is a by-product of systemic proliferation, and where a site is a systemic circumstance, 'everything is architecture'. There is no exterior, because there is nothing else.

Convolutedness takes this circumstantial instability as an opportunity to produce increasingly fluid interactions between decision-making environments and to mediate between them with an evolving normativity. Its virtual megalomania is an expansive sieve that operates beyond the division between the real and the possible. It manoeuvres between potentials, transverses disparate scales and puts together domains whose coexistence cannot yet be conceived. In this domain all relationships are malleable. Time can be collapsed or expanded as if it were infinitely flexible and available. This megalomania carries a growing potential of operation, which remains abstract without being reductive, virtual without being ideal and ubiquitous without being Utopian.

Latency: The Double Delay

Better yet, it is the quasi-stable turbulence that a flow produces, the eddy closed upon itself for an instant, which finds its balance in the middle of the current and appears to move upstream, but is in fact undone by the flow and re-formed elsewhere.
MICHEL SERRES, 1982[5]

Turning the perpetual drift towards chaos inside out, convolutedness is the agent of unpredictability. Its movement constitutes a temporary stability, creating a latent and transitory knowledge that unfolds as a radical practice. Disorder is reversed by deviation and turned into complex distribution. Convoluting architecture follows deviation. A bundle of

5 Serres (1982), p. 75.

divergent times converges in its temporary knot and becomes coordinated. 'Negentropic islands in the entropic sea.'[6] Convolutedness evolves out of a noneternal standstill, in a mixture of delay and agility.

Prior to the production of any material organization, convolutedness introduces itself in the temporal continuum: it makes a sudden leap into duration, single-mindedly guided by any line of information, motivated by difference, driven by pattern stimuli, under a cautiously inclusive attitude and a fabricated short memory. This leap requires the simple move of systematically dissolving spatial categorizations under performative parameters. It recalls a virtual (transhistorical) memory for its operation. It populates this latency through more or less relaxed (into space) or contracted (into duration) series of preorganizational planes: an ontological 'hesitation' that it inflates or deflates depending on the urgency with which it operates. For this purpose and in this context, it segregates temporal scales and alters their duration. Long-term processes are shrunk into instantaneous sections of time, short moments are expanded. Through this first delay, a plane of latency is traced. This plane is a qualitative multiplicity made up of algorithms, differential rhythms and active patterns. Unlike the spatial legends of *tabula rasa* and site-specificity, this plane is neither blank nor contextual, both being spatial categories.

Instead of flattening abruptly the virtual into the actual in order to fulfil a sudden effect on reality through shock (the most effective device to sustain the shallow robustness of a representational system), convolutedness performs a second kind of delay: it delays actualization by suspending judgement (even indefinitely) and by dissipating representation in numerous exchanges of information within its virtuality. It makes itself available as a field of negotiation, a protocol open to multiple inputs. It becomes a kind of suspended and collective abstract expressionism. The second delay operates as a conservative impulse that increases intensities in the virtual by forcing the proliferation of interactions between domains and by unfolding and cascading their effects: convolutedness deepens virtual codependence. It operates as an abstract mind over any individual one and proliferates collective desires. It engineers aura.

The double-delay, and the extravagant pragmatism this involves, creates an opportunistic deferral of architectural action. It works under the assumption that a localized management

6 Serres (1982), p. 73.

of efficiency in the responses of a system has the potential to release emissions containing both wider extents and higher levels of performance. It increases redundancy by multiplying single-mindedness. This form of pragmatism exhaustively decodes names, conventions, typologies and objects into smaller components, into attributes, into relationships and finally into performances. In a system of this kind, many ratios (cause-effect relationships) stand for a rationale (comprehensive system of belief). But these ratios are taken one by one, as if the system could not think too many things at the same time, as if it had the capacity to provisionally forget. Its expediency and straightforwardness are so extreme that, paradoxically, they do not account for many levels of practicality. This initial simplicity becomes complex as new demands are integrated into it through dumb rules of adaptation. It becomes systematically creative: the more locally reasonable, the more globally unreasonable. Its modus operandi is based on short memory. It barely has a method. It rather creates method along its trajectory of incorporation of problems. In this sense the system only pretends to forget. Its structure is the by-product of its course of action. Its procedure is its contingency-orientated route. The compulsive production of formulae replaces here any underlying principle, any totalizing basis. There is no foundation. There is only motivation. The producer occupies a space of absolute uncertainty and freedom all at once, without even deciding it. In such a space, a new kind of cohesiveness needs to be built in.

Operativity: Machinic Levels

The healthy system … may be compared to an acrobat on a high wire. To maintain the ongoing truth of his basic premise ('I am on the wire'), he must be free to move from one position of instability to another, i.e., certain variables such as the position of the arms and the rate of movement of his arms must have great flexibility, which he uses to maintain the stability of other more fundamental and general characteristics. If his arms are fixed or paralyzed (isolated from communication), he must fall.
GREGORY BATESON, 2000[7]

The many planes of latency constitute a single plane, one that is fluctuant and without boundaries, a plane of consistency that upgrades affiliations in the relational sets. A machinic regime is constituted by this technically consistent self-management: an ecology that steers

7 Bateson (2000), p. 507.

virtual capabilities. At least four levels participate in this ecology: firstly, the constitution of modalities of mediation of the processes of determination; secondly, the integration of these modalities into a manifold of determination; thirdly, the engineering of the system's devices of sensitivity to its own emergent patterns; and finally, the constitution of learning-to-learn capabilities.

On the first level, a machinic regime requires the engineering of simple devices of mediation. Mechanistic models have historically aimed at reducing the relationship between cause and effect to one where the effect can fully explain the cause. This reversibility has progressively detached determination from creation, encapsulating one in a predictable arena and the other in a magical one. But while magic is just a particular form of causality, the effects do not always explain the causes, as in a logical chain. When they do, it is only in hypothetical isolation. Moreover, the very basic module of any process of differentiation is precisely the difference between cause and effect, or change. Determination is actually this difference in itself. Very basic levels of culture have been constructed upon the knowledge or denial of this difference, the smallest declination of matter. The first level of a machinic regime implies the construction of cause-effect relations or modalities of differentiation: qualitative and quantitative variations in the inputs associated with qualitative and quantitative variations in the outputs. They engender a system's creativity.

On the second level, these modalities are integrated into increasingly complex chains, where effects operate as causes. As these chains cascade, they trigger iterations in which the same cause-effect relationship reenters the system. Diverse domains enter into operative coordination, and are forced to exchange information. The chain takes its modalities beyond their initial precision. They interact in a protocol of exchange, where forces are not just resisted or mediated, but where they mediate each other. These sequences of change engender richness and intensify or balance potentials.

On the third level, learning capabilities are bred into the system, in order to integrate the sequences of change into intelligent bundles. The system learns to use the same forces that produce change in order to change change. The system becomes sensitive and responsive to its own effects. This sensitivity is embedded in the rule system through the insertion of evaluations and new responses. External conditions are absorbed. They sediment hierarchies between the chains and introduce larger contexts of operation. This level involves the engineering of a first degree of learning: what habits the system will establish, what kinds of change it will allow and to what degree. It engenders the intelligence of the system.

The fourth level diversifies this intelligence. Tighter or looser strategies result from the ability of a system to adjust the hierarchy and configuration of its chains of change to what it learns. This level allows fluctuation between complex potentials. The system learns to learn. Through the management of learning, it becomes more or less self-contained and more or less conservative, determining where and when habits are adopted and where and when changes are allowed. This constitutes the flexibility of the system to regulate its intelligence.

Aesthetics: The Economy of Abundance

The economics of the system, in fact, pushes organisms towards sinking into the unconscious those generalities of relationship which remain permanently true and towards keeping within the conscious the pragmatics of particular instances.
GREGORY BATESON, 2000[8]

The fifth level, which overwrites all the others, is constituted, on the one hand, by the mood of the system, the tightness of its frame of mind, its global generosity and its grace; and on the other by its fitness and ability to survive. Both are by-products of its accumulation of surplus, understood as a particular excess of performative dimensions. Both lead, ultimately, to its durability and construct its particular mode of artificial duration. Through an incessant process of iteration, it manages the superfluousness of potentials as a collective redundancy to be steered and deposited. It is mostly in this sense that it operates as a confabulation of determination against itself. Determination complexifies and takes the form of a particular mode of robustness. The aesthetics of a system are the consequence of its economy. At this level, a system negotiates the allowance or disallowance of change with forces so unpredictable and intangible that they are traditionally replaced by a metaphysical or ideological apparatus. But these forces work simply on a different level: a fluent and rapidly fluctuant temporality that appears as an elusive simultaneity. These forces work at many coexisting degrees of collectivity (human and nonhuman), because they work through and across many

8 Bateson (2000), p. 142.

degrees of consciousness, or better, virtuality. They communicate in a domain that lies before procedure and infrastructure, and far beyond ideology. In this milieu, which spans cultures and levels of consciousness, organization blurs with communication. It becomes a mesh of abstract messages, a memory operating at a genetic level. In this multiconscious continuum, and being unceasingly striated and interfered with by the stoppages of convention, a system enters into dialogue with times that are much beyond our life span (the life span of an individual or of a collective awareness). It reaches extremes of volatility that can only be approached directly between virtual levels rather than through action- or theory-orientated levels of consciousness.

The economy of a system is determined by the management of its manifold potentials. Tight economies, which tend to relate to single-minded relational sets, end up provoking fast decadence. Curiously, however, it is sometimes precisely because of this deterioration that they are able to survive. Generous economies usually leak too much; they expend too much energy and they collapse. But in provoking acceleration, they occasionally summon a potential future. These 'anticipations' ensure their survival. Sometimes perished economies survive because of their rareness, and secure ones surprisingly die or become frozen because they are taken for granted and devalued into a habit. A convoluted system is a delicate balance of times. Its aesthetics have to do not only with its configuration, not even just with its performance, but also with its change of performance. It is by offering multiple sides and edges, and by generating richness, that a system becomes capable of changing its function and adapting.

No trace of modernistic determination remains here. Its pragmatics and ideology are radically changed without falling into criticality. Work manifests itself as an unpredictable yet specific chain of reactions that tame and add cohesiveness to the virtual, concentrating and spreading the intensity of its driving forces. While mechanical work is aimed at surrendering wilderness under a purposive human control, machinic work is the discovery of potentials and the production of new directions within the systemic wilderness, without the need of sense. Beyond discourse, eternity, universals or transcendence, convolutedness is consistent senselessness.

Addressing the absence of a theory of convolutedness is architecture's most urgent enterprise. Without a theory of convolutedness, architects are left in the difficult position of trying desperately to adjust to an absurd conversation in which the parameters are constantly changing. Without convoluted thinking, architecture remains a subset of history and keeps postponing its broader historicity, renouncing its innovative potential and confusing its condition as a 'vehicle of modernization' with a mere desperation for stimulating modernity through the image. Without convoluted thinking, architecture degrades into a form of media by swallowing semantically (and pretentiously) the speed of changes, by repressing material differentiation and expression in the comfortable replication of a formal convention with a prefigured meaning.

The aesthetics of the shock on which this ethics is based have become simply boring, a repetition of hopeless gestures to attract attention, shallow and idealistic at the same time. Its effects are culturally, socially, environmentally and economically less enduring. The architect-warrior is again drawn into politics, into the propaganda machine of mass culture. Why would we continue this insistence on the image? What for? The myth of the ephemeral is merely a dissipation of the specificity of our work. In this sense, there is probably no possibility of a theory of convolutedness without a practice. Yet practice has to be redefined in a broader sense: as a technical enrichment towards a wiser approach to production. Because there is no theory of convolutedness, we do not yet know how to follow the virtual without asking sooner or later about some sort of legitimacy. We do not know how to sustain the movement without a ground, how to continue working without explaining. We do not know how to 'carry' culture instead of just 'talking' to it. Because there is no persistent following, most practices quickly collapse under their self-awareness: they systematize themselves discursively, and then they die. A fashionable shift comes later. 'Architecture or Revolution' might be claiming this principle of survival: increase the ability of the discipline to cope with complexity, or die in a quasi-revolution. How convoluted can architecture get?

In order to integrate itself productively in this context, architectural theory has to assume that the notion of the virtual stops being vague, and develops into an abstract and rigorous operativity. It is challenged to cut across planes of latency with more planes, by introducing higher degrees of awareness in the relational sets, by interfering actively with their performance, by seducing them, by producing deviations and stoppages. For this purpose, it probably needs to intensify its exchanges with vaster ecologies and become itself ecological, in the most abstract sense. Architectural theory is required to embrace dynamics beyond and before the human. It is challenged to dissect architectural specimens without reducing them to the crystallized particularity of a timeless generalization or a short-term historicity. It is compelled to study species, to trace lineages, to measure affinities, to determine modes, rates and patterns of change and to evaluate emergent performances. Theory has to account for the making of difference itself. Recognizing discontinuities, anomalies, mutations, trends and transitions becomes more important than the identification and isolation of identities or the search for essential characteristics, generalizations or regularities. History acquires here a problematic continuity with evolution itself, as it obtains the active power to intensify an emergent collective consciousness by integrating ever-higher degrees of awareness into the abstract learning levels of culture. The historical material needs to be reformulated under this expanded form of history. A whole jargon and new classification systems have to be borrowed, negotiated and appropriated.

If there is an architectural discipline as such emerging out of this panorama, it is in the construction of an operativity of the oscillation into and back from the virtual. Although no 'ultimate' condition of architecture can be foreseen or preconceived, there probably are visions without the eyes and thoughts before the brains. Convolutedness invokes profound and systematic modes of intuition, methods to leap, tactics to delay and linger, and techniques to explore and expand the virtual. Convolutedness has no content as such. It is pure form: the creation of a form to handle time in its hesitation. A vigorous eagerness to participate in the tremendous uncertainty of the future and a remorseless irresponsibility for the perplexities of the past are the only seepages from the paradoxes of retrospective meaning and of prospective projections. Convolutedness in architecture blurs prejudices about the reduction of the discipline to a false science, a form of anthropology, a poor geology, a material economy, a flat ecology, a quick biology or a clumsy meteorology, into a slow process of disciplinary empowerment, with the ingenuous and harmless good old purpose of taking over.

Architecture's release from the pressure of representation has yet another level to populate and rationalize. Culture has only achieved this level in certain domains where the conditions of production have pushed the practice across the threshold of mere relevance into the realm of pure and direct emotion. By systematically renouncing high forms of the practice, or better, by assigning increasingly instantaneous success to its low forms, the standards of production of some artistic practices exploded rapidly and exponentially, producing both proliferation and true immediacy.

Beyond certain speeds, a material practice acquires the sudden properties and the passionate regime of 'flickering': a frantic state of sudden agitations. At its highest speeds, a system fluctuates before any capture is possible. The difficulty in broaching flickering is the apparent randomness emergent from its speed. But flickering is the result not of capricious behaviour, but intense acceleration. It seems incredible that increasing the rate of oscillations in and out of the virtual can produce such singularities in the material unfolding, in a way that desire becomes capable of triggering new forms of nonideological will. It seems even harder to accept that these singularities invent a rationale of their own, slippery forms of order through excess of consistency. Of all possible categories, flickering cannot accept a manifesto. It is itself pure manifestation. Delayed by the machinic through its currently necessary obsession with procedural rigour, technical precision and control over the chains of cause and effect, its immanent aesthetics are ignored as an 'impossible task'. But in fact, only flickering engages the regimes of complexity to the point of merging intelligence with emotion, through undomesticated yet precise cultural actions.

Architecture has blocked the possibility of access to this level of environmentalism through its paradoxical anxiety about power. This condition is beyond liquefaction: it is the self-vaporizing of the practice into absolutely smooth transitions. It is not just transformation but rather aggression without violence. It touches where it hurts and leaves immediately. Architecture is still too slow to incorporate these properties. They sound metaphorical. Yet the activation produced by flickering is literal, as much as the effective consumption of energy it propagates and the passion it unfolds. It is both pure physicality and pure virtuality. Continuity is taken by flickering to a point of discontinuity: ubiquitous climax. The virtual and the actual are collapsed by speed. A rave. A riot. No distance between action and effect. Trance. Fear.

Flickering convolutedness, the material regime of the absolute sudden, is the evidence that architectural acceleration will, sooner or later, furiously burn the virtual in an environmental momentum. By doing this, architecture will silently propagate its forces directly into our senses. Without ever looking back at the ruins, we are fatally attracted to acceleration, carrying the historical materials on our back as virtual potentials; throwing them into convolutions; and ultimately burning them.

176

Mohsen Mostafavi has been Chairman of the Architectural Association since 1995. Formerly Director of the Master of Architecture 1 Program at the Graduate School of Design, Harvard, he has also taught at the University of Pennsylvania, Cambridge University and the Frankfurt Academy of Fine Arts (Städelschule). Recent publications include *Approximations, Surface Architecture* and *Logique Visuelle.*

Ciro Najle, head of the AA's graduate programme in Landscape Urbanism and a Diploma Unit Master, has been a design critic at Columbia, Cornell, the Berlage Institute and the University of Buenos Aires. He worked in New York with Reiser+Umemoto and K Easterling, and has practised independently since 1991.

Iñaki Abalos and **Juan Herreros** practise architecture in Madrid, with projects throughout Spain and Europe. Both are professors in Madrid's School of Architecture, and have also held positions at Columbia and the AA, among others. They are authors of the books *Le Corbusier, Skyscrapers, Tower and Office* and *Natural-Artificial.*

Lawrence Barth is a writer and a lecturer in the Graduate School of the AA, where his primary academic interests revolve around the intersection of urbanism and political theory. He is also a consultant urbanist, collaborating regularly with architects on urban-scale projects, including the urban strategy for the recently completed One-north masterplan in Singapore with Zaha Hadid Architects.

Architect **Florian Beigel** runs the Architecture Research Unit and is a senior lecturer in the department of architecture and spatial design at London Metropolitan University. Recent work with **Philip Christou**, also of ARU, includes 'A Second Nature Landscape in Cospuden', a plan to regenerate landscapes and communities destroyed by strip mining in Germany. Beigel is the author of *Time Architecture* and *Caravanserai.*

James Corner is Chair and Professor of Landscape Architecture in the Graduate School of Fine Arts at the University of Pennsylvania, and with architect Stan Allen is partner of Field Operations, based in Philadelphia and New York.

Michel Desvigne, of Desvigne & Dalnoky, is a landscape architect working in Paris. A regular collaborator with architects such as Renzo Piano, Richard Rogers and Norman Foster, Desvigne is known for projects such as the urban park at Issoudun (Indre) and the TGV station and viaduct at Avignon. He has taught at the ENSP in Versailles, the Polytechnic in Lausanne and the Architectural Institute in Geneva.

Keller Easterling is an architect, teacher and writer. Currently Assistant Professor of Architecture at Yale, she is the author of *Organization Space: Landscapes, Highways and Houses in America* and *American Town Plans,* and co-author of *Call It Home,* a laserdisc history of American suburbia from 1934 to 1960. Easterling's work has been exhibited widely. She has taught design and history at Parsons School of Design, the Pratt Institute and Columbia.

Michael Hensel is a partner in Ocean North, a Helsinki-based practice that undertakes experimental design in combining architecture, urban design, product design and cultural production. A founding member of the do-group, Hensel teaches at the AA. Recent publications include *Contemporary Processes in Architecture* and *Contemporary Techniques in Architecture.*

Designer and critic **Christopher Hight** is Assistant Professor at Rice University's School of Architecture. In addition to teaching at the Architectural Association, he has worked for the Renzo Piano Building Workshop in both Paris and the US, and has published widely.

Detlef Mertins is Associate Professor and Director of the Graduate Programme in Architecture at the University of Toronto. He was Professional Adviser for the Downsview Park Competition in Toronto, Canada, the results of which are published in Julia Czerniak, ed., *CASE: Downsview Park Toronto.*

Jesse Reiser and **Nanako Umemoto** have practised in New York City as Reiser+ Umemoto RUR Architecture since 1986. Reiser currently teaches at Princeton. RUR has built projects at a wide range of scales, from furniture design to residential and commercial structures, up to landscape design and infrastructure.

Alejandro Zaera-Polo, founding partner, together with Farshid Moussavi, of Foreign Office Architects in London, is Dean of the Berlage Institute. He has taught at, among others, the AA, Columbia, Princeton, Yokohama University and UCLA. FOA's first major commission was the Yokohama International Ferry Terminal, Japan, which opened in 2002.